the NAUGHTY SECRETARY CLUB

jennifer perkins

the NAUGHTY SECRETARY CLUB

THE WORKING GIRL'S GUIDE TO HANDMADE JEWELRY

jennifer perkins

NORTH LIGHT BOOKS

CINCINNATI, OHIO

www.mycraftivity.com

12 11 10 09 08 5 4 3 2 1

Distributed in Canada by Fraser Direct
100 Armstrong Ave.
Georgetown, ON, Canada L7G 5S4
Tel: (905) 877-4411

Distributed in the U.K. and Europe by David & Charles
Brunel House, Newton Abbot, Devon, TQ12 4PU, England
Tel: (+44) 1626 323200, Fax: (+44) 1626 323319
E-mail: postmaster@davidandcharles.co.uk

Distributed in Australia by Capricorn Link
P.O. Box 704, Windsor, NSW 2756, Australia
Tel: (02) 4577-3555

Library of Congress Cataloging-in-Publication Data

Perkins, Jennifer.
  Naughty Secretary Club : jewelry for the working girl / by Jennifer Perkins. – 1st ed.
    p. cm.
  Includes index.
  ISBN-13: 978-1-60061-116-2 (alk. paper)
  1. Jewelry making. 2. Kitsch. I. Title.
  TT212.P466 2008
  739.27–dc22

2008000795

EDITOR: Jessica Gordon
DESIGNER: Karla Baker
PRODUCTION COORDINATOR: Greg Nock
ART DIRECTOR—PHOTOGRAPHY: Marissa Bowers
PHOTOGRAPHERS: Ric Deliantoni, Al Parrish, Christine Polomsky
STYLIST: Lauren Emmerling

dedication

To my mother, who is my patron saint of craft, the wind beneath my crafty wings and the person I consult before making a single crafty move. I love you so much that if you think about it too hard your head will explode.

fw
F+W PUBLICATIONS, INC.
www.fwpublications.com

METRIC CONVERSION CHART

TO CONVERT	MULTIPLY	BY
Inches	Centimeters	2.54
Centimeters	Inches	0.4
Feet	Centimeters	30.5
Centimeters	Feet	0.03
Yards	Meters	0.9
Meters	Yards	1.1
Sq. Inches	Sq. Centimeters	6.45
Sq. Centimeters	Sq. Inches	0.16
Sq. Feet	Sq. Meters	0.09
Sq. Meters	Sq. Feet	10.8
Sq. Yards	Sq. Meters	0.8
Sq. Meters	Sq. Yards	1.2
Pounds	Kilograms	0.45
Kilograms	Pounds	2.2
Ounces	Grams	28.3
Grams	Ounces	0.035

about the author

Jennifer Perkins is the head honcho behind the kitschy jewelry business Naughty Secretary Club (www.naughtysecretaryclub.com).

Her work has been featured in major newspapers and magazines, including *Marie Claire*, *Lucky*, *BUST*, *Teen Vogue*, *The New York Times* and more. Appropriately enough, she started her company while working as a secretary. (She was being naughty by making jewelry when she should have been answering phones.)

In addition to Naughty Secretary Club, Jennifer is a founding member of the Austin Craft Mafia (www.austincraftmafia.com), which now has branches across the United States. Along with other members of the Austin Craft Mafia, Jennifer co-produces Stitch (www.stitchaustin.com), Austin's largest indie fashion show and craft bazaar. As if this wasn't enough to keep her busy, Jennifer also hosts *Craft Lab* and co-hosts *Stylelicious* on the DIY Network.

When Jennifer is not working, which is not often, you can find her at her aqua home in South Austin with her husband, Chris, their cat, Georgie, and their dogs, Lucy and Ella. When she's not at home, she's most likely at a flea market, out having Tex-Mex or on a friend's porch with a cold drink in her hand.

PHOTOGRAPH BY *Cory Ryan*

acknowledgments

When it comes to business, there is no such thing as luck, but there is such a thing as supportive and inspiring friends and family.

When I was a wee little girl, my mom, Fredda, always encouraged me to craft and be creative. She let me dress myself and pick out my own outfits.

My father, Dan, who—bless his heart—is not so crafty, does have a great mind for business. I remember my dad teaching me the word *entrepreneur* as we sat on the beach during one of our family vacations. "Jennifer," he would say, "you need to always work for yourself, rather than working to put money in other people's pockets." These words stuck with me.

My younger sister, Hope, who got the actual artistic talent, never ceases to amaze me with her endless creativity. She is the mastermind behind Phoning Flo (page 56) and all the other office-hottie illustrations in the book.

Also, thank you to my wonderfully tolerant and supportive husband. Chris never complains about the jewelry parts all over our house or about my saying "craft" and "vintage" at least twenty times per day.

Thank you to the amazing ladies of the Austin Craft Mafia—especially Vickie Howell for always wearing my jewelry. To Lisa Sichi for listening to me ramble and offering great advice. To *BUST* magazine for giving me the feature that let me quit my day job. Also thanks to Kathy Cano Murillo and Traci Bautista for pressuring me into writing a book in the first place. Thank you to my wonderful editor, Jessica Gordon, for being so patient with me on my first time around in the book-writing world.

contents

Introduction 8
Job Skills 10
Supplies and Tools 12
Secretary School 18

A CASE OF THE MONDAYS 22

Office Hanky-Panky **Jewelry Set** 24
Thank You for Calling **Bangles** 30
Pencil Pusher **Necklace** 34
Shredded Junk Mail **Bangles** 36
Shredded Junk Mail **Necklace** 38
Jot-'Em-Down **Earrings** 40
Ravishing Receptionist **Sweater Clips** 42
Paper Clip **Necklace** 46
Binder-Folder Bling **Necklace** 48
Clickity Clack **Shoe Clips** 52
Phoning Flo **Necklace** 56

HUMP DAY 60

Whistle at Work **Necklace** 62
Quitting Time **Headband** 64
Transfer Me **Jewelry** 70
Secretary's Delight **Bracelet and Ring Set** 72
Pink **Collar** 78
Clock Watcher **Necklace** 82
Copy Machine **Necklace** 86
All-Access Pass **Badge Holder** 90
Tied Down **Brooch** 94
Tin Typewriter **Bracelet** 98

TGIF 102

Happy Hour **Charm Bracelet** 104
Casual Friday **T-Shirt Necklace** 108
Hotel Key **Necklace** 112
Secretary's Pad **Necklace** 114
Secretary's Day Bouquet **Bracelet** 120
To a Great Secretary **Necklace** 124
Specs Appeal **Necklace** 126
Typewriter-Ribbon Tin **Necklace** 132

Patterns and Pictures 136
Everybody's Blogging for the Weekend! 138
Resources 139
Unlikely Sources 140
Index 142

on being a naughty secretary...

If you prefer your jewelry subtle and serious, you might want to go ahead and set this book back on the shelf. However, if kitschy accessories made with a wink and a smile are your cup of tea, then *The Naughty Secretary Club* will have you on the edge of your chair.

As a preview of this jewelry adventure, let me share the backstory of how I got into making jewelry and what ultimately influenced the projects on the following pages. It all really started when I was a wee little girl and my parents dragged me to flea markets and antiques stores every weekend. My dad collected Bakelite radios, so to pacify my sister and me they suggested we collect Bakelite jewelry. This eventually expanded to all kinds of costume jewelry, and now I have a room in my house with the walls and shelves covered in it.

But readymade jewelry was never quite tackaliscious enough for my taste. Like a mad jewelry scientist, I found myself tearing up the jewelry and putting it back together again to better suit my style. I wanted jewelry that was bigger, sillier and sometimes even functional. I won my fourth-grade science fair with a pair of earrings I made with a travel-sized toothbrush and bright pink plastic beads hanging from one ear and matching beads and travel-sized toothpaste hanging from the other. Being a young enterprising designer, I thought maybe I could supplement my allowance with a little jewelry designing. Not a bad idea in theory, but I decided to use slimy worm-shaped fishing lures as my medium of choice. This was ultimately my downfall. On a warm spring day, the wormy earrings would stick to my customers' faces and hair. I was soon searching for a new bauble to hang on an ear hook. Through the years nothing has been safe when it comes to jewelry. I have encased small doll heads in resin, drilled baby rattles for pendants and cut up old books for graphics with wild abandon. Sure, beads are great and all, but as you should see by now, I go for the more obscure.

If this brief little history of my foray into jewelry making strikes a chord with you, then we are going to get along just fine. Jewelry is supposed to be fun and whimsical and make you happy. It should reflect your personality. The main thing I ask myself when I am creating a one-of-a-kind piece is, "Does this make me giggle?" If I can answer yes, then I have done my job. Remember, even if some of the projects in this book are not exactly your style, the techniques you will learn can be tweaked into the project of your dreams… Even if your dreams don't involve doll heads and cupcake toppers—although I can't imagine why not—you can take what you learn and make something that does float your boat.

JOB SKILLS

Some projects in this book are harder than others, just like in the working world—making a spreadsheet is harder than sending a fax, you know. All the projects are identified by difficulty level. Keep in mind, however, that practice makes perfect, and it is jewelry making, not rocket science. So with a little overtime you can make anything in this book!

FIRST DAY ON THE JOB:

Even on the first day of the job, you know how to use a pair of scissors or a tube of glue. You could make all of these projects before your first cup of coffee at the office.

YOU DESERVE A RAISE:

You work hard for your money, so hard for it, honey, and your jewelry prowess shows it! These may be a little tougher, but still no hill for a stepper.

RUNNING THE SHOW:

At this point, you are the boss, bomb-diggity and belle of the jewelry ball. You are making executive decisions in the blink of an eye about things like resin and metal files. For these projects, you probably will need to study the instructions carefully. A little practice before you plow right in also might be a good idea. But don't let this scare you, for you, too, have the right stuff to become an executive administrative assistant.

TRADiTiONAL
jewelry-making supplies

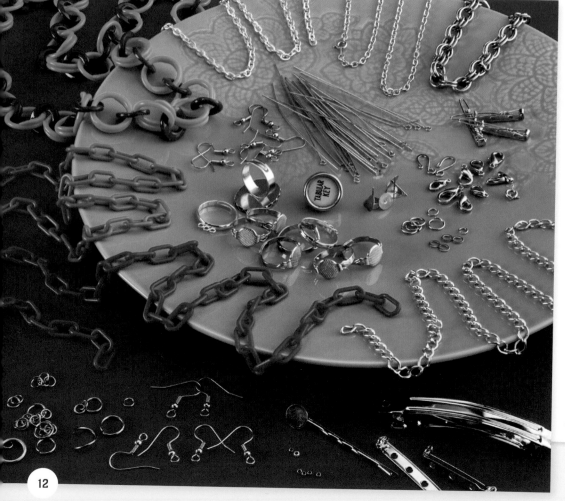

CLOCKWiSE FROM TOP LEFT: *colored plastic chain, metal chains, head and eye pins, pin backs, lobster clasps, hook-and-eye clasps, jump rings, earring posts, ring blanks, ear hooks, barrette and bobby pin blanks, crimp beads, more ear hooks, more jump rings.*

Although I make a point of using nontraditional supplies, there are a few must-have items for any jeweler. Always have these items handy. Nothing will drive you to happy hour overindulgence more quickly than being halfway through a project and realizing you are short that one crucial item.

JUMP RiNGS: These metal rings come in all shapes, sizes and colors. I find it handy to have almost every kind. You never know when you are going to need a wee brass jump ring or a ginormous silver ring.

HEAD PiNS: I love head pins, and I am not afraid to shout it from the rooftops. Head pins are long, thin pieces of wire with a little base on the bottom. I love them because you can use them to make almost anything into a charm—and who doesn't love charms?

Here's a tricky point about using head pins. The holes in older vintage beads are often larger than the head pin's base, so the beads will slide right off, possibly leading to a mental health crisis. When this happens, I scrounge around in my carpet and find a runaway seed bead and slip that on the head pin first. This little bead acts as a stopper for the larger hole of the old bead, keeping it on the head pin.

EYE PiNS: A close relative of the head pin, the super-handy eye pin has a small loop at the bottom instead of a flat base. Eye pins are often used to connect beads to other things. Sometimes you use the eye pin to connect a wire-wrapped bead to another bead to make a chain of beads. I often use eye pins when making earrings so I can slip on a bead and then use the loop at the bottom to attach a tassel or charm. Some people prefer to get wire and make their own head and eye pins. I am not that kind of gal. Why go to the hassle when you can buy them readymade?

* A note about head pins and eye pins: Naughty Secretary Club jewelry is not about precise measurements and calculations. I take a fairly one-size-fits-all approach when it comes to findings. All head and eye pins referenced throughout the book are 21-gauge 3" (8cm) long base metal. Or substitute whatever you like best.

CHAiN: Chain is a fun item to incorporate into jewelry. There are traditional chains in all colors, thicknesses and types, with names like snake and cable. Of course, I prefer the colorful thick plastic chain. Sometimes I am fortunate enough to find vintage jewelry chain, but other times it just takes a trip to the local pet or hardware store to score great colors. Investigate both for their selection of plastic and metal chain. Who knew parrots found bright-colored plastic chain such an amusing toy?

CLASPS: Toggle, lobster, hook-and-eye? No, this is not a secret jewelry language—these are different styles of clasps. In most cases, selecting a clasp is totally a matter of preference and depends on the project. For instance, sure a lobster clasp is a sturdy choice for a bracelet, but good luck getting that baby on your wrist alone. For bracelets, most designers opt for a toggle clasp, which is very easy to fasten when primping alone. Toggle clasps also are used often for necklaces, although personally I am a hook-and-eye kind of gal. When choosing a clasp, be sure to think about what is easiest for the person wearing the jewelry. We have all been there alone, toiling fruitlessly in sweaty frustration. Then you are classically conditioned to hate that bracelet, so alone and sad it sits in your jewelry box, never to be worn again.

JEWELRY WiRE AND CRiMP BEADS: If you are making a traditional beaded necklace, you will need both wire and crimp beads, generally speaking. Jewelry wire comes in spools at your craft store, and you choose a style based mainly on the weight of your finished project. When choosing just the right crimp bead, you want to be sure you have chosen a bead with a hole large enough to accommodate a double thickness of your chosen jewelry wire.

other personal favorites...

EAR HOOKS: Add a charm or a bead on a jump ring, head pin or dangle to one of these little metal hooks to make super-fast, super-fabulous earrings.

EARRiNG FLAT PAD POSTS, BLANK BRACELETS, BLANK BOBBY PiNS AND BARRETTES: Use strong glue to adhere a pretty little something to the flat blanks on these pieces.

OFFiCE POTLUCK:
a little of this and a bit of that

FROM TOP LEFT: *gnome on plastic tubing, T-shirt, vintage typewriter, swizzle sticks in stamp carousel, old ties, doll furniture, vintage children's glasses, toy calculator, vintage time card and clothespin, phone cord, doll couch with vintage button pillow, jar of vintage goodness, watch bands, beads, paper clips, vintage beaded chain, tin squares and other random stuff.*

I like beads as much as the next guy, but there is much more to jewelry than just beads. I look at everything as a possible piece of jewelry, no matter how big or small. When you see something that catches your eye based on color or style, think to yourself: "Could this be drilled and made into something else? Could pieces of it be used to make a new piece of jewelry?" More often than not, the answer is yes.

The Naughty Secretary Club: The Working Girl's Guide to Handmade Jewelry takes this philosophy to a whole new level. It's like when you have a potluck at your office. There seems to be a little of everything there on the conference room table. Well, think of random piles of supplies in the same way. Seven-layer dip and sesame noodle salad might not sound like a great gourmet pairing, but together they are quite the yummy hole filler. Several of the supplies I use for jewelry are a bit on the unusual side. They might not seem like an awesome combination, but you just have to trust me on this.

CUPCAKE TOPPERS: Everyone loves cupcakes, especially inspired jewelry designers. Lick the icing off the cupcake topper, and use your drill to make a couple of holes. Presto, it becomes a pendant.

TELEPHONE CORDS: Curly cord is archaic anyway—you might as well put it to good use. Hit the thrift store looking for old phones with brightly colored coils you can weave around bangle bracelets.

CHILDREN'S EYEGLASSES: Just make sure they are not in use by some poor kid before you make them into jewelry. Tear the arms off, hit them with the drill, fill the lenses with resin—they will never correct vision again when you are done with them, but they will make a dang cute necklace.

PAPER CLIPS: They're handy to have in your desk drawer as well as in your jewelry supply kit. Linking embellished paper clips together is so easy, you'll never even have to leave your desk.

TIN TYPEWRITERS: There is no need to stop playing with toys at any age. Cut apart these vintage toys so you can wear them as jewelry.

MEN'S TIES: These are no longer for the boss man after you cut them up and run them through your sewing machine.

PLASTIC TUBING: Embrace your inner plumber and hit the tubing aisle to make a few bangle bracelets.

SWIZZLE STICKS: Happy hour is not just a social activity. It is now a hunt-and-gather mission. Cut the fun bits off swizzle sticks and incorporate them into your jewelry.

T-SHIRTS: And you thought you couldn't wear them to the office. Maybe not as shirts, but as necklaces, yes.

SHREDDED PAPER: One secretary's trash is another secretary's treasure—all you need is a bit of découpage medium and a willingness to get your hands dirty.

Oh yeah…and a few **BEADS:** There is truly a never-ending supply of beads in all colors, sizes and shapes imaginable. I especially love vintage beads.

HOT TIP

Not only should you use your imagination when it comes to choosing supplies—you should also consider unlikely techniques. Could jewelry be sewn, embroidered or découpaged? You bet your paycheck it can.

BASIC TOOLS
what a crafty girl needs

FROM TOP LEFT: *clear tape, various adhesives, high-speed drill with various attachments and bits, scissors, heavy-duty wire cutters, chain-nose pliers, round-nose pliers, flush cutters, chain-nose pliers, round-nose pliers.*

You can have all the cute findings, beads and funny charms you want, but if you don't have the right tools, sister, you're going nowhere fast. I actually don't use a lot of fancy tools when I make jewelry. I'm not sure I have ever had a pair of crimping pliers in my hands. The tools listed here are the things I do use almost every day.

CHAIN-NOSE PLIERS: These pliers have flat pincers, and they are handy as all get-out for twisting your jump rings (remember: never pull them apart) and squishing crimp beads. They can fill in as a third hand, as well.

ROUND-NOSE PLIERS: The rounded pincers of these pliers are perfect for making loops when wire wrapping.

JEWELRY WIRE CUTTERS: As tempting as it is to use your desk scissors on jewelry wire, don't. First, they really don't work that well, and second, you'll ruin your scissors. These special little cutters are sometimes referred to as flush or side cutters. They are exactly what you need to clip off excess bits of head and eye pins as well as to cut your beading wire.

HIGH-SPEED DRILL AND WOOD BLOCK: The adventurous jewelry designer will need a good drill. Drills come with different-sized bits and accoutrements. You can make a pendant from a piece of broken plate by using a ceramic bit to drill a hole, and you can shape wood or metal with a variety of sanding bits. Standard drills generally won't hold bits as small as a jeweler needs, so a high-speed drill is invaluable. The wood block goes under the piece you are drilling so you don't poke a hole in your desk when the drill goes through the other side of the item being drilled.

* *A note about drill bits:* I am really not a stickler for using a "correct" size of drill bit. Generally speaking, I use two bits—a small one and a bigger one. All bits are listed in this manner. You pick the bit that's right for you.

HOT TIP

When gluing unlikely things together (like a metal ring base and a slick plastic button), sand the back of your button first to rough up the surface, or give it a little "tooth." The glue will adhere much better.

GLUE: If glue were a person, we totally would have matching best-friend rings. I use glue all the time when making jewelry, including in the projects throughout this book. The glue aisle can be overwhelming, but if you stick with a nice hardy glue like E-6000 or clear urethane glue (like Liquid Fusion) you will be all right. There also are special glues for working with fabric or wood.

SCISSORS: Paper collage is an easy technique that most people don't associate with jewelry making, but they should. Small scissors with sharp points are best for cutting out small designs from paper. If you sew, don't use any of your sewing scissors for cutting paper. It will dull them quickly. Use scissors designed to cut paper. You'll find them in the scrapbooking aisle of craft stores.

SECRETARY SCHOOL

There are no techniques in this book that require formal training. I have a degree in psychology—not jewelry making—and I designed and made all these projects. So can you. The main qualifications for this job are a bit of creativity and a strong attraction to kitsch.

MAKING A WRAPPED LOOP

Wire-wrapped loops are as fundamental to jewelry making as the sentence "The quick brown fox jumped over the lazy dog" is to a person studying for a typing exam. With the help of a drill, an eye or head pin and this technique, almost anything can be transformed into a charm.

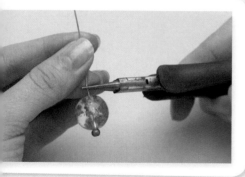

1 GRASP HEAD PIN WIRE WITH PLIERS

Slide a bead or beads onto a head pin (or eye pin). Grasp the pin about ⅛" (3mm) above the bead with round-nose pliers. The higher above the bead you grasp, the more wire wrapping you will do. Also, the size of your loop will vary based on how close to the tip of the pliers you hold the wire. The closer to the tip you hold the wire, the smaller the loop. I recommend eyeballing it on the smaller side.

2 CREATE LOOP

Making a wrapped loop is much easier if you start with a longer head or eye pin. This also allows you to use bigger beads (hooray!). Use your fingers to bend the wire around one of the pincers of the pliers. If you have not yet developed calluses or find the metal difficult to bend, feel free to use another pair of pliers rather than your fingers.

3 WRAP WIRE AROUND BASE OF LOOP

Use your fingers (or pliers) to wrap the wire around the base of the loop and down the shaft of the head or eye pin. Wrap the wire snugly so the coils are flush with each other. Keep wrapping until you reach the bead. If you start wrapping too high above the bead, you'll end up with a long, wrapped neck between the bead and the loop. It will take some practice to gauge how far above the bead you should start.

4 TRIM WIRE

Use flush cutters to trim off any excess wire left from wrapping.

5 FINISH LOOP

If necessary, use your chain-nose pliers to tuck away the end of the wire.

OPENING AND CLOSING A JUMP RING

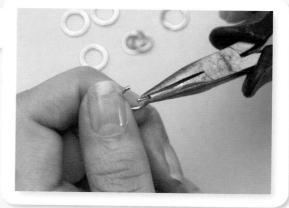

There is a right way and a wrong way to open and close a jump ring. Doing it the wrong way is sure to get you fired before you finish your first week on the job.

Jump rings are cut at an angle, so if you pull them apart they will never fit back together correctly. Always twist them from side to side to open them. To open a jump ring, hold it between your thumb and index finger on one side of the break. Grasp the other side with chain-nose pliers just beyond the other side of the break. Twist the jump ring so you are pushing one side and pulling the other in a lateral motion. Hook the jump ring to the project and then close it using the opposite motion. In a best-case scenario, the jump ring will make a light clicking noise as the two sides meet. That is your little pat on the jump-ring back that you have done a good job.

THINGS YOU CAN DO
with a high-speed drill

If you want to turn poker chips into pendants and dice into charms, a high-speed drill with the right bits is invaluable. High-speed drills are generally much smaller than regular drills, making them much easier to handle for small-scale work. They turn at a high rate of speed, producing clean, neat holes. Most importantly for the jewelry maker, they also will hold much smaller bits than a regular drill. When learning to use a high-speed drill, practice on scrap pieces first, and be sure to drill on top of a wooden block so you don't ruin your tabletops.

Drills generally have settings for variable speeds. (The speed refers to how fast the bit turns.) You may have to set the speed before beginning to drill, although high-end drills are controlled by a foot feed similar to the foot control for a sewing machine. In that case, the speed is controlled by how hard you press the foot feed. High-speed drills also may have a flex shaft. This is a flexible arm attached to the drill with the bit at the end. It can be held much like a pencil. High-speed flex-shaft drills are often seen in nail salons, where they are used with a sanding bit rather than with a drill bit. Before buying a high-speed drill, be sure to do your research to determine which drill will work best for you.

Bits are the different devices that fit into the end of the drill. There are all kinds of bits for all kinds of needs, including cutting, sanding and drilling, of course.

CLOCKWISE FROM BOTTOM LEFT: *cutting wheel, sanding tools, flex-shaft high-speed drill on top of wood block, various bits.*

SANDING

A wee little bit of sandpaper affixed to a high-speed drill can work wonders to smooth a surface. Your drill will come with a special bit and replaceable tubes of sandpaper that fit it.

DRILLING

The most common bit and the one most often used by a jeweler to make a hole is the twist bit. It is a small, round metal rod with a point at the end and a winding groove that twists up the shaft. The point makes the hole, and the groove carries the waste produced by the drill up and away from the hole. Bits are made of different metals, and you should use the type best suited for the material you are drilling. This is especially important when drilling through metals. Bits come in standard sizes, and although it is not necessary to use the same brand of bit as your drill, you always should refer to the manufacturer's information on the type and size of bits best suited for your drill. It is a good idea to keep a variety of sizes and types of twist bits so you'll have the size you need.

MAKING A CHARM OR PENDANT

Use a high-speed drill to make any plastic piece into a pendant or charm. Here, I am drilling through a vintage plastic cake topper with a smaller bit.

DRILLING THROUGH RESIN

Once you've created your resin masterpiece, you'll often need to put some holes in it so you can incorporate it easily into your jewelry. When drilling through resin, always wear a mask. Resin dust is not so awesome for your lungs or eyes. Resin also can be brittle, so drill slowly and steadily. Pull your drill in and out quickly and frequently as you drill, as if stabbing at the resin piece. This motion gives the resin time to cool. You also may drip a little water into the hole as you drill.

HOT TIP

Remember, you must always wear safety goggles when using any type of drill, especially when cutting or sanding.

A CASE OF THE MONDAYS

Mondays, unlike paydays, come around way too often. They're the kind of days you need to ease into. You don't want to tax your brain by taking on any really complicated projects. You generally want to stay away from problems like creating world peace or curing the common cold. Great breakthroughs just don't happen on Mondays. The first day of the week is the kind of day when you make necklaces out of paper clips (see page 46) and pen caps (see page 34) as you daydream about what happened Saturday night. Let's face it, no real work ever happens on a Monday.

The epitome of office culture is the iconic image of cute gals gabbing on the phone. When preparing for a good gab, you always remove one earring so you don't hurt your ear with the phone. Many an earring has been lost due to this telephone ritual. Now those singles can find use again. Vintage hankies, stray clip-on earrings, telephone charms and more come together in this project for a little Office Hanky Panky.

OFFICE HANKY-PANKY
jewelry set

skill level:
FIRST DAY ON THE JOB

TAKE A MEMO

Office romance has been around as long as there have been, well, offices. According to the 2007 Vault Office Romance Survey (www.vault.com), if you suspect some hanky-panky in your office, you're probably right. Here are the cold, hard facts:

· 42% of those surveyed had an office romance.
  Love is in the air.

· 11% would have a romance if they could.
  Now that's just sad.

· 19% dated a boss or other superior.

· 19% had a tryst at the office. But wait, it gets worse…

· 17% were caught having a tryst at work!
  Talk about getting caught with your pants down!

· 20% met their spouse or significant other at work.
  Love conquers all.

· 23% had an "office" husband or wife—a platonic friend they spent time with regularly.

· 48% who had an office romance hid it from everyone.
  The best way to keep a secret is not to tell it.

· 36% knew of an office romance in their workplace.
  So much for keeping that secret.

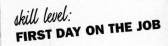

SIGN HERE

STUFF YOU'LL NEED

*1 hanky or other thin vintage fabric scraps
(1 hanky makes the main project plus all variations)*

3 vintage clip-on earrings

silver bracelet blank

button-covering kit

chain-nose pliers

wire cutters

scissors

clear urethane glue (Liquid Fusion)

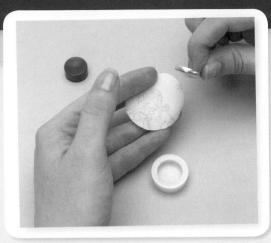

1 GATHER MATERIALS

Choose a hanky or other piece of thin material with an office-themed image. This hanky shows teenage girls on the phone, but when the individual images are made into buttons all you see is the telephone imagery. Gather stray vintage clip earrings that match or coordinate, a bracelet blank, glue, scissors and a button-covering kit. Make sure the size of the button-covering kit you choose will fit on the glue pads of your bracelet blank.

2 PREPARE TO COVER BUTTON

Using the circle template provided in the button-covering kit, cut out a circle from your hanky, making sure the part of the image you want to show is in the center of the circle. Hold the fabric circle right-side down and center the top half of the button on top of it.

3 ARRANGE COVERED BUTTON INSIDE CUP

Insert the fabric with the top half of the button on top into the larger plastic cup. Fold all the extra fabric edges on top of the button. Push the back of the button into the plastic cup, making sure all the fabric edges are tucked under it.

4 SECURE BUTTON BACK

Use the cap provided in the cup to push the button back down into the plastic cup, securing the fabric under the button back. Simply pop the covered button out of the plastic cup.

5 REMOVE BUTTON SHANK

Use chain-nose pliers to remove the shank from the back of the covered button.

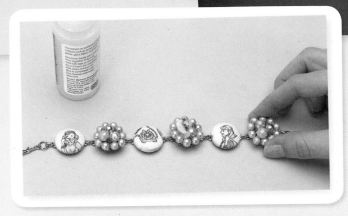

6 **REMOVE BACKS FROM CLiP-ON EARRiNGS**

Use chain-nose pliers and wire cutters to remove the backs of the vintage beaded clip-on earrings.

7 **ADHERE COVERED BUTTONS AND BEADED EARRiNGS TO BRACELET BLANK**

Apply clear urethane glue to the back of the first hanky-covered button and adhere it to the first bracelet blank. Next adhere a clip-on earring. Alternate between covered buttons and beaded earrings until all the blanks are filled. Allow the glue to dry.

EXTRA *goodies*

No need for the fun to stop with the bracelet—make an entire matching set! Vintage advertising phone charms make smashing earrings, a fabric-covered button adheres to an adjustable ring back to make an adorable ring, and a covered button adhered to a pink plastic disc and hung from chunky blue plastic chain makes a great necklace. Coordinating jewelry is an important staple in office-appropriate attire!

Button-Covered Necklace

Button-Covered Ring

Button-Covered Earrings

BUTTON-COVERED *hair ties*

STUFF YOU'LL NEED

elastic hair ties

button-covering kit

vintage fabric scraps

Why should your hair be left out of the button-cover party? For this accessory you can use any size button cover you want. This also is a great way to use up all your fabric scraps. Just remember: You don't want to remove the button shank like you did for the jewelry.

Remove the shank to make cute button-cover bobby pins!

1 SLIDE ELASTIC THROUGH BUTTON SHANK

Cover a button with a scrap of vintage fabric. Fold an elastic hair tie in half and thread the doubled end through the button shank.

2 SECURE HAIR ELASTIC

Pull the other end of the elastic through the loop you made and tighten it.

SPELL-CHECK *bracelets*

STUFF YOU'LL NEED

6 letter tiles for each bracelet (or old button for ring)

bracelet blank (or ring blank for ring)

E-6000 glue

Rack up points with your boss and coworkers by wearing these witty office-themed game-tile bracelets. Since they're so easy to make, you'll have enough to give to everyone at the holiday office party this year.

Think of your six-letter word, gather up the appropriate letter tiles and glue them into place on the bracelet blanks. Allow them to dry.

WE NEED A RAISE *ring*

Keep an eye peeled for old pins at flea markets and antiques shops. Pop the pin finding off the back and glue a ring blank in its place. You'll get your message across without even having to go on strike.

TAKE A MEMO

Here are some more work-related six-letter words to choose from— or make up your own!

Payday

Minion

Worker

Office

Honcho

Employ

29

Anyone who has ever answered an office phone for his or her boss knows these words by heart: "Thank you for calling (insert company name here). How may I direct your call?" That was my spiel for years. Some days I said that sentence so many times I wanted to rip the phone cord right out of the wall. Now that I think about it, that's kinda what I did to make this bracelet.

THANK YOU
FOR CALLING
bangles

SIGN HERE

skill level:
FIRST DAY ON THE JOB

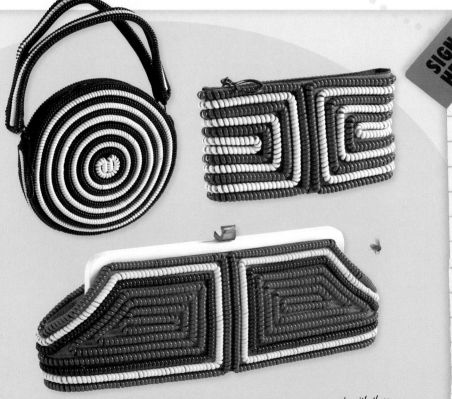

For years, I have been picking up items made with these vintage coils. Here are a few from my collection.

STUFF YOU'LL NEED

$^3/_4$" (2cm) clear plastic tubing

phone cord coiling in various colors

wooden dowel rod to fit inside plastic tubing

E-6000 glue

high-speed drill with cutting attachment

scissors

clothespins

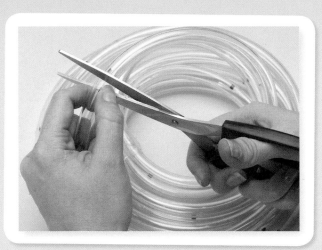

1 MEASURE AND CUT TUBING

Wrap one end of the tubing around your wrist and mark the point where you want to cut the tubing. The bangle should be large enough to fit over your hand. Cut the tubing with scissors.

2 CUT DOWEL ROD

Use a high-speed drill with a cutting attachment to cut a small piece of dowel rod. You want the rod to be just long enough to insert into both ends of the plastic tubing, about 1½" (4cm).

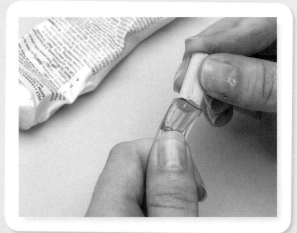

3 ADHERE DOWEL PIECE INSIDE TUBING

Pinch one end of the tube closed about ½" (1cm) from the end and squirt a bit of E-6000 into the tube. Slide the dowel rod piece into the tube. Repeat with the other end of the tubing and the other end of the dowel rod.

4 SECURE DOWEL INSIDE TUBING

Secure the ends of the plastic tubing with a clothespin. Allow the glue to dry for several hours or overnight.

5 WRAP PHONE CORD AROUND TUBING

When the glue is dry, remove the clothespin and begin wrapping the phone cord around the bangle shape. You might have to manipulate the phone cord a bit to adjust for gaps. The goal is to cover the bangle entirely and see as little plastic tubing as possible.

6 SECURE PHONE CORD

Apply some E-6000 to the cut end of the phone cord and secure it with a clothespin. Allow it to dry overnight.

PHONE CORD *earrings*

I combined unusual vintage beads made to look like phone cord tubing and covered buttons with flower charms to create these unique flapper earrings.

PENCIL PUSHER
necklace

SIGN HERE

STUFF YOU'LL NEED

1 vintage fountain pen

1 silver eye pin

1 readymade silver tassel

1 readymade 18" (46cm) silver necklace chain

selection of small vintage charms

selection of small beads

small jump rings

high-speed drill

chain-nose pliers

round-nose pliers

wire cutters

skill level:
YOU DESERVE A RAISE

Just because a 1940s celluloid fountain pen hasn't seen ink since World War II doesn't mean it won't make a great piece of jewelry. These fountain pens are easy to find at flea markets and at online auction houses. They come in great muted colors and sometimes in swirls and stripes. For the adorable necklaces they make, they are worth the search!

1 DRILL HOLE IN PEN CAP

Gather all your materials, including a selection of charms and beads to go with your choice of silver or gold metal. Use a 1/16" (2mm) bit to drill a hole directly through the very top of the pen cap.

2 LINK TASSEL TO EYE PIN AND THREAD THROUGH PEN CAP

Open the loop at the top of the premade tassel with chain-nose pliers and slide it onto the eye-pin loop. Thread the eye pin through the hole in the pen cap. Make a wrapped loop in the eye-pin wire where it extrudes from the pen cap. (See page 18 for instructions on making a wrapped loop.) Cut off any excess wire. The eye pin should be pulled up far enough that the eye-pin loop is not visible from beneath the pen cap.

3 ADD CHARMS

Use small jump rings and chain-nose pliers to add charms to your tassel. You also can add beads wire-wrapped into a charm. Repeat for as many charms and beads as you would like on your tassel.

PENCIL
on a ball chain

When searching for old fountain pens, also keep an eye out for vintage bullet pencils. Named for their shape, bullet pencils make great necklace pendants, too. Many were printed as souvenirs or advertising tchotchkes and come pre-drilled or with a built-in loop at the top. All you have to do is string the pencil onto a necklace chain!

SHREDDED JUNK MAiL
bangles

STUFF YOU'LL NEED

premade bangle bracelets

old magazines and junk mail

découpage medium

clear waterproof topcoat

sponge brush (optional)

skill level:
FIRST DAY ON THE JOB

more
paperwork,
please

Oh, and the fun doesn't have to stop with just bangles. Look through your jewelry box for other baubles that need a paper-coated face-lift.

Almost every office has a shredder, and after a morning of shredding junk mail, catalogs and old magazines, you will have a bountiful batch of colorful shredded goodness. Grab your découpage medium and plain bangle bracelets and get started making eco-friendly bling from that mountain of recycled paper.

1 ADHERE SHREDDED PAPER TO BANGLE

Shred your junk mail (or colorful magazines). Spread a bit of découpage medium onto the bracelet using your fingers or a sponge brush and begin adhering bits of shredded paper. Apply the paper strips randomly; just be sure to overlap the shredded paper in a continuous layer.

2 FINISH BANGLE

Allow your découpaged bangle to dry overnight. Once it's thoroughly dry, take your bracelet outside or into a well-ventilated area and apply several coats of a clear, water-proof topcoat. Découpage medium tends to get tacky in humid conditions, and the topcoat will prevent that from happening. You can't go deep-sea diving in your new bangle, but with a good topcoat it should not get tacky when you wash your hands, either.

Now make a second one, then a third and fourth. Bangles always look better when worn stacked, and there is no shortage of shredded paper!

CRUMPLED PAPER *brooches*

When paper does not make it to the shredder, just crumple it into a ball and play trash-can basketball instead. Dig those crumpled balls out of the trash and make yourself a pretty little flower brooch. Glue your three circles together at the center, then glue a button or fun cabochon in the center. Glue a pin back to the back of the brooch.

SHREDDED
JUNK MAIL
necklace

skill level:
YOU DESERVE A RAISE

Jewelry as environmentally conscious as it is fashionable—does life get any better? Reach into the office shredder for a handful of color, and hit your craft stash for some felt. Now découpage the paper onto wooden beads and cut the felt, and you are on your way to a unique one-of-a-kind necklace.

These earrings totally shred. A matching pair of earrings insures that "everyone is on the same page."

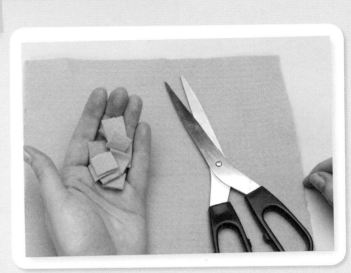

1 COVER BEADS WiTH SHREDDED PAPER

Shred junk mail (or colorful magazines) and adhere the paper shreds to each wooden bead with découpage medium, overlapping the pieces of paper until each bead is covered entirely. Allow the covered beads to dry completely. Once the beads are dry, give them at least 2 coats of clear spray paint. Allow the paint to dry completely. Use your drill with a bit the size of your bead hole to poke through the paper covering each bead hole. Repeat with all your beads.

2 CUT FELT SQUARES

Cut a sheet of light blue craft felt into ½" (1cm) squares.

3 STRiNG NECKLACE

Attach one end of a length of stringing wire to a crimp bead. Thread the free end of the wire onto a sewing needle, and string the necklace in the following sequence: red seed bead, black-and-white polka-dotted bead, red bead, felt square. Simply bring the needle through the center of the felt squares to string them. Repeat the sequence 11 more times, ending with a black-and-white bead. Then thread on 7 découpaged beads, alternating with black-and-white beads. Repeat the sequence from the first side, beginning with a black-and-white bead. Finish the necklace by attaching the free end of the wire to a clasp with a crimp bead. Link the other clasp component to the other end of the wire with a jump ring.

JOT-'EM-DOWN
earrings

skill level:
FIRST DAY ON THE JOB

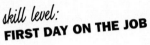

Just like a Boy Scout, a good Naughty Secretary is always prepared to take a memo, even if it means taking that memo with her earrings. Readymade plastic hoop earrings and pencil charms pair up for earrings you could use to take dictation, mark your bowling scores or play hangman on a long flight.

A girl can never have too many no. 2 pencils around.

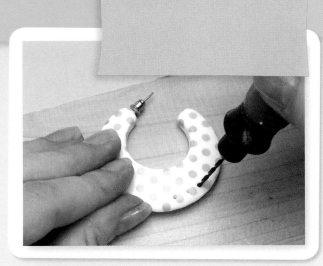

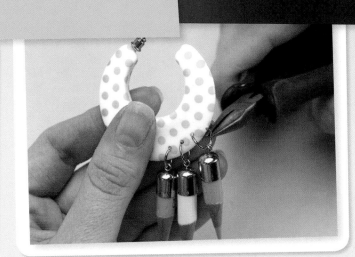

1 DRiLL HOLES iN PREMADE HOOP EARRiNGS

Use a high-speed drill and a small bit to make 3 holes along the bottom of a premade hoop earring. (See page 21 for instructions on drilling with a high-speed drill.) Repeat for the second earring.

2 LiNK PENCiL DANGLES TO EARRiNGS

Open a jump ring with chain-nose pliers and slide a premade pencil charm onto it. Slide the jump ring into the first hole in the earrings. (See page 19 for instructions on opening and closing a jump ring.) Link the remaining dangles to the earring, and repeat for the second earring.

RULER
bracelet

Why stop with pencils? All kinds of office supplies, like jointed rulers, make great jewelry. Wrap the ruler around your wrist and remove any extra links so the ruler fits. Drill holes on either side of the bracelet. Add a clasp with jump rings and pliers.

The office can be a cold, foreboding place—and I mean that quite literally. The first line of defense for the office ice age is to have a cardigan at the ready. Why should your office mates see you in that same black/white/fill-in-the-blank sweater day after frigid day when that dowdy cardigan could be adorned with an adorable set of sweater clips? Whether it's bacon and eggs or a telephone, a cheery sweater clip will make that plain-Jane sweater seem new and different every time you don it.

RAVISHING RECEPTIONIST
sweater clips

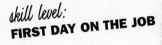

SIGN HERE

skill level:
FIRST DAY ON THE JOB

FILE
sweater clips

STUFF YOU'LL NEED

sheets of stiffened craft felt in various colors

red and blue round flat-back glass cabochons

premade sweater clips

scissors

paper

pen

fabric glue

Ordinary binder clips snagged from a desk drawer and attached to chain with a jump ring make for a unique spin on the sweater clip.

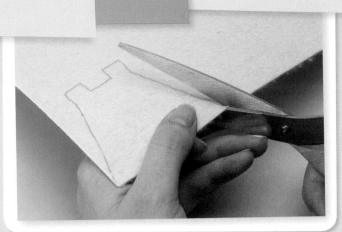

2 CUT OUT FELT TELEPHONE

Use fabric scissors to cut out the telephone shapes.

1 TRACE TEMPLATE ONTO FELT

Photocopy the telephone template on page 136 onto a sheet of sturdy paper and cut it out. Trace around the template on the felt with a pen.

i HEART YOU
sweater clip

Send a super-stealth message to your office crush when you wear this clip with your favorite sweater set.

3 GLUE DETAILS ONTO TELEPHONE

Cut out a black circle and a slightly smaller white circle from craft felt to create a telephone dial. Also cut out small black strips for bands on the receiver part of the telephone. Adhere the face and the bands to the telephone with fabric glue.

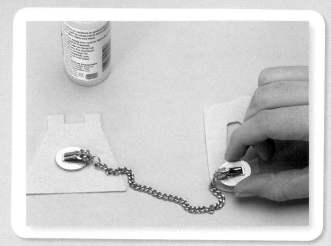

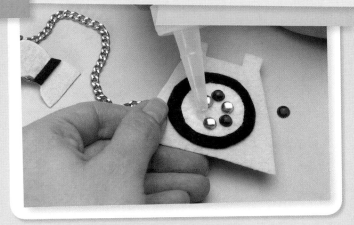

5 GLUE ON FLAT-BACK GLASS GEMS

Use fabric glue to adhere red and blue flat-back glass gems to the telephone dial. Allow the glue to dry.

4 ADHERE CLIPS TO TELEPHONE PiECES

Glue each telephone piece to one of the clips with fabric glue. Allow the glue to dry.

ViNTAGE *sweater clip*

STUFF YOU'LL NEED

approx 5" (13cm) beaded chain

2 6mm silver jump rings

2 aqua plastic telephone charms

alligator clips

E-6000 glue

Glue an alligator clip to the underside of each telephone charm, making sure that the side of the clip that opens and grabs the sweater points away from the charm hoops on the plastic phones. After the glue has dried, link the 2 telephones together with a 5" (13cm) length of beaded chain and 2 small jump rings.

Vintage advertising telephone key chain charms make the perfect sweater clips for any ravishing receptionist.

PAPER CLIP
necklace

STUFF YOU'LL NEED

25 smaller paper clips in assorted colors

14 larger paper clips in assorted colors

colorful paper (Traci Bautista)

double-sided tape

clear glue

scissors

skill level:
FIRST DAY ON THE JOB

Paper clip necklaces are a venerable tradition passed down through generations of bored-to-tears office workers. Combine your favorite scrapbooking paper (or junk mail) with a few supplies you already have in your desk drawer, and your new necklace will be dry and ready in time for happy hour.

The inspiration for my paper clip necklace is this groovy version made with contact paper that I found at a flea market.

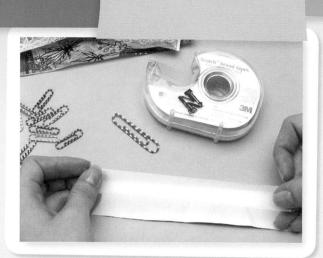

1 ADHERE DOUBLE-SIDED TAPE TO PAPER STRIPS

Cut a sheet of colorful paper into 1" (3cm) wide strips. Place the paper face down on your work surface and adhere a strip of double-sided tape along the entire length of the paper.

2 WRAP PAPER CLIPS iN PAPER

Cut each strip down to approximately 2" (5cm) long (size depends on the paper clips you use). Wrap 1 piece of paper around a larger paper clip, making sure to leave space at both ends for linking.

3 SECURE PAPER AROUND CLIPS

Apply dots of white glue along one edge of the piece of paper and fold it into place, covering the paper clip. Repeat steps 1 through 3 until you have made 11 paper-covered paper clips.

4 LiNK PAPER CLiPS iNTO NECKLACE

Link the paper clips together, alternating between smaller plain and larger paper-covered clips. Once you have used all the paper-covered clips, link the chain into a necklace with a final plain paper clip. Link together several short paper clip chains at the center to create a tassel.

While cruising through my local office supply store, I was struck with a jewelry-making epiphany: Plastic folders and binders are really jewelry masquerading as office supplies. Both come in oodles of bright, yummy colors, and it seems like such a shame to relegate them to some file drawer. They are crafty goodness just waiting to be transformed. I used circles, flowers and hearts, but since this thin plastic is so easy to cut, the sky's the limit on what you can design.

BINDER-FOLDER BLING *necklace*

skill level:
FIRST DAY ON THE JOB

HEART *earrings*

If you heart filing more than anything in the whole wide world, then let everyone know with these earrings!

STUFF YOU'LL NEED

plastic file folders in multiple colors

assorted decorative brads

silver chain with lobster clasp

6mm silver jump rings

scissors

small hole punch

decorative-shape paper punches (optional)

chain-nose pliers

1 CUT CiRCLES FROM PLASTiC FiLE FOLDERS

Cut 4 approximately 2¼" (6cm) diameter circles from the plastic file folders. I cut 1 circle from each of 4 different colored folders. Then cut 12 approximately 1" (3cm) diameter circles from the plastic file folders, choosing the color combination you like best.

2 PUNCH HOLES AND BEGiN TO LiNK CiRCLES

Use the hole punch to make a hole in each side of each larger circle. Punch a hole directly in the center of each smaller circle. Slide a brad through the holes in 1 of the smaller circles and 2 of the larger circles, making sure the small circle is on top of the 2 larger circles. Flatten the brad's posts at the back of the circles to connect them.

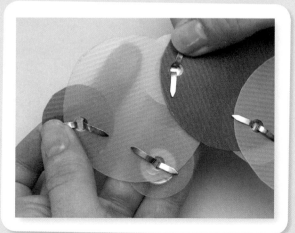

3 CONTiNUE LiNKiNG LARGE AND SMALL CiRCLES

Once the 4 large circles are linked, punch a few more holes in the large circles and add 5 more small circles, making sure to place 1 small circle at either end of the main pendant section where the chain will be linked.

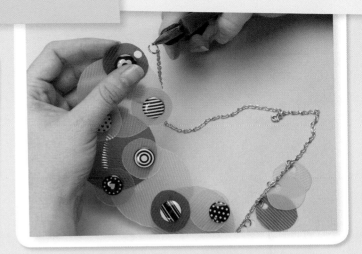

4 PUNCH HOLES FOR CHAiN

Punch a hole in each of the small circles at either end of the main section to accommodate the chain.

5 ADD CiRCLE DANGLES AND CHAiN

Punch a hole at the top of each of the 4 remaining small circles. Link each one to the chain with a jump ring, beginning approximately 2" (5cm) from one end and spacing the dangles about 7 links apart. Link each end of the chain to each small circle with a jump ring. (See page 19 for instructions on opening and closing a jump ring.)

FLOWER *brooches*

Use your file folder scraps to make fun and festive flower brooches! All you'll need are pin backs you can find at the craft store to glue to the back.

Sure, when you walk to work you sport the ever-fashionable tennis-shoes-with-skirt look. You probably make Coco Chanel roll over in her grave, but hey, a gal has to be sensible. Sorry, Coco. However, once you are at the office, it's a whole other story. There is just no good reason why those fancy shoes stashed in your desk drawer should not be accessorized.

CLiCKiTY CLACK
shoe clips

TAKE A MEMO

When I was an administrative assistant, I often walked to and from work. Often, because my salary didn't afford me much in the way of lunch, I would walk through downtown Austin during my lunch hour. Just as important as the tennis shoes I kept under my desk during working hours for these jaunts was my MP3 player loaded up with inspirational music. Here are a few of my favorites:

"9 to 5" *by Dolly Parton*

"Take This Job and Shove It" *by Johnny Paycheck*

"Step into My Office, Baby" *by Belle and Sebastian*

"Take a Letter Maria" *by R.B. Greaves*

"A Secretary Is Not a Toy" *by Frank Loesser*

"She Works Hard for the Money" *by Donna Summer*

"Working for the Weekend" *by Loverboy*

"Morning Train" *by Sheena Easton*

"Manic Monday" *by The Bangles*

"Welcome to the Working Week" *by Elvis Costello*

"Career Opportunities" *by The Clash*

SIGN HERE

STUFF YOU'LL NEED

1 spool of zebra-print wired ribbon

2 3" (8cm) diameter wooden discs

2 shoe clips

2 miniature plastic typewriters

clear urethane glue (Liquid Fusion)

scissors

1 SECURE ONE END OF RiBBON WiRE

Cut about 6" (15cm) of zebra-print ribbon. Locate one of the wire ends and pull it out a bit. Bend the wire end into a hook so it will catch the end of the ribbon when you begin to pull the wire out of the ribbon at the opposite end.

2 PULL WiRE OUT OF RiBBON AT OPPOSiTE END

Begin pulling the wire out of the ribbon at the opposite end to where you secured the wire in step 1, bunching the ribbon up as you go. Continue pulling out the wire until the ribbon bunches up into a circle.

3 ADHERE RiBBON CiRCLE TO WOODEN DiSC

Cut away any excess ribbon with scissors. Adhere the ribbon circle to one of the wooden discs with clear urethane glue. Allow it to dry.

4 ADHERE TYPEWRITER TO CENTER OF RiBBON

Adhere the typewriter in the center of the ribbon circle with clear urethane glue. Allow it to dry. Adhere the typewriter-and-ribbon decoration to a shoe clip with Liquid Fusion. Repeat steps 1 through 4 to make the second shoe clip.

TYPEWRITER KEY
shoe clips

Before that first cup of coffee, figuring out which shoe goes on which foot can be quite a feat—left and right shoe clips come in handy on those days. But let me take a moment for a brief safety message. If you are having difficulty with left and right and you are running late, I strongly suggest taking the bus. Neuropsychological issues and stress can make driving particularly hazardous in the morning. Just a little Naughty Secretary Club Life Tip.

STUFF YOU'LL NEED

2 old typewriter keys (*L* and *R*)

2 black buttons large enough to accommodate the typewriter keys with a border

2 white poker chips

2 shoe clips

clear urethane glue (Liquid Fusion)

high-speed drill with cutting attachment

1 CUT AWAY BACKS OF KEYS

Use the high-speed drill with the cutting attachment to remove the metal backs of 2 vintage typewriter keys. I chose the letters *L* and *R* for obvious reasons.

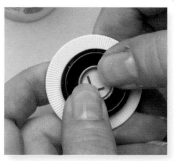

2 FINISH SHOE CLIPS

Glue a button to the right side of the poker chip and glue a letter key on top of the button. Adhere a shoe clip to the back of each poker chip with clear urethane. Allow the glue to dry.

Phoning Flo is everyone's dream secretary. She has a towering coif unrivaled in the office world, a Texas tattoo, platform shoes and enough green eye shadow for the whole office. Oh, and let's not forget her hot pink typewriter. My guess is she is telling whoever is on the other end of that phone line to kiss her grits.

PHONING FLO *necklace*

skill level:
YOU DESERVE A RAISE

STUFF YOU'LL NEED

1 4¼" x 3" (11cm x 8cm) oval wooden disc

1 sheet of scrapbook paper with typewritten letters

decorative secretary image (see image at left)

gold-tone tassel bead

approx 28" (71cm) gold-tone chain

2 10mm gold-tone jump rings

lime green acrylic paint

découpage medium

sparkly découpage medium

Diamond Glaze adhesive

pencil

paintbrush

deckle-edge scissors or other fancy-edge scissors of your choice

scissors

high-speed drill with small bit

wood block

chain-nose pliers

1 PAINT DiSC AND CUT SCRAPBOOK PAPER iNTO OVAL

Give the wooden disc 2 coats of lime green acrylic paint on both sides. Allow each coat to dry completely. Photocopy the image of Phoning Flo on page 57. You may need to change the size of the picture to fit your wooden disc. Cut around Flo in an oval shape approximately ½" (1cm) smaller than the wooden disc. Cut an oval from the scrapbook paper with typewritten letters that's slightly larger than the secretary oval, using deckle-edge scissors or pinking shears.

2 ADHERE PAPERS TO DiSC

Apply découpage medium to the wooden disc and center the larger oval on top. Apply another layer of découpage medium and center the secretary image on top of the larger oval. Apply a final layer of découpage medium over the entire disc and allow it to dry.

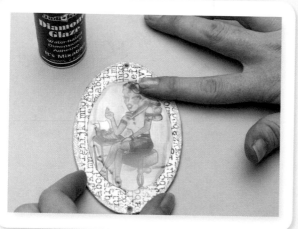

3 APPLY FiNiSHiNG COATS

Carefully apply a coat of sparkly découpage medium to the typewritten paper border. Allow it to dry. Then apply a coat of Diamond Glaze on top of the secretary image. Allow it to dry.

4 DRILL HOLES

Use a high-speed drill and a larger bit to drill a hole at the top center and bottom center of the découpaged wooden disc, approximately ⅛" (3mm) from the edge of the disc. (See page 21 for instructions on drilling with the high-speed drill.)

5 LINK CHAIN AND TASSEL TO PENDANT

Add a large 10mm gold-tone jump ring to the top of the pendant and run the gold chain through the ring. Using the other gold jump ring, attach the premade tassel bead to the hole drilled in the bottom of the pendant.

HOT TIP

Chain can get quite expensive the minute you label it "jewelry chain." Sure, if you are into chichi jewelry and need solid gold or sterling chain, by all means hit the jewelry supply joints. However, if you are a person of modest means and prefer cheap and chic, do not overlook your friendly hardware store. You can buy chain in all kinds of colors and sizes at your neighborhood Home Depot or Lowe's. It looks like the same base metal chain to me, but for some reason when it is not called jewelry chain it is a lot cheaper. Oh, and another hot tip about chain: Don't overlook those $.99 necklaces in the display case at the thrift store. That is raw chain begging to be recycled.

HUMP DAY

Hump Day is like the old saying about a glass of wine: Is it half full or half empty? The optimist would say the workweek is half over, and the pessimist would say there is still half a week to go. Let's be optimistic and say that by Wednesday you have recovered from the weekend and you've started to get your work groove on. You are ready to take on larger projects because you are not completely burned out yet. You are in the middle of climbing that proverbial workweek hill, and the same could be said for jewelry challenges. At this point, you won't blink an eye at metal files (see page 98), liquid UTEE (see page 86) or embroidery (see page 90).

WHiSTLE AT WORK *necklace*

STUFF YOU'LL NEED

3 small plastic gnome cake toppers

12 large blue-and-white-polka-dotted plastic beads

2 small blue-and-white-polka-dotted plastic beads

approx. 11 vintage plastic flowers (some larger than others) to layer or use with beads

6 small beads for flower centers

6 gold-tone charms to dangle from flowers

30 green plastic disc beads

18 small round orange plastic beads

approx. 22" (56cm) stringing wire

1 gold-tone S clasp

6 gold-tone eye pins

6 4mm gold-tone jump rings

2 gold-tone crimp beads

chain-nose pliers

high-speed drill with very small bit

wire clippers

skill level:
YOU DESERVE A RAISE

Gnomes have a work ethic like no others'. We should all really look up to them, except they're so short we'd have to look down, which defeats the whole purpose. I digress. They are always pictured doing some sort of gardening involving tools like rakes and hoes, but they are never without a smile plastered across their faces. I made this necklace so that when things are getting a little stressful and overwhelming at work, I can think WWGD (What Would Gnomes Do)? The gnomes would, of course, smile, whistle a happy tune and plow right through those mountains of paperwork on their desks.

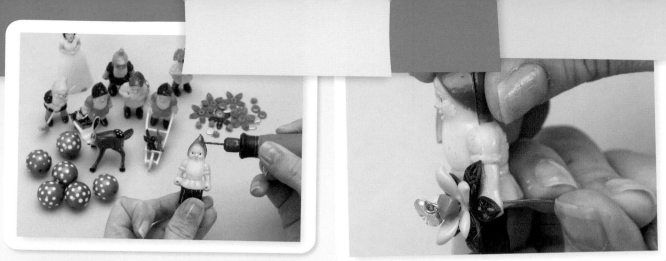

1 DRILL HOLES

Use the high-speed drill and a very small bit to drill a hole through each gnome's hat. The cake topper gnomes may have holes in their hands already, but if not, drill a hole in each hand. (See page 21 for instructions on drilling with a high-speed drill.)

3 STRING NECKLACE

Slide 1 crimp bead onto 1 end of the 22" (56cm) of stringing wire, then thread the wire through 1 of the clasp components and back through the crimp bead. Flatten the crimp bead with chain-nose pliers. String the necklace in the following order: green disc, orange bead, green disc, large blue-and-white bead. Repeat this sequence until you've used 6 blue-and-white beads, ending with an orange bead. String on the first gnome, followed by an orange bead, a green disc, a small blue-and-white bead, green disc, orange bead, second gnome. Repeat this sequence until you've strung on all 3 gnomes. String the remainder of the necklace in the same sequence as the first half, beginning with an orange bead. Crimp the second clasp component to the end of the stringing wire.

2 MAKE BOUQUETS

Link a charm to an eye pin with a jump ring. (See page 19 for instructions on opening and closing a jump ring.) Slide on a small bead, a smaller flower and a larger flower, stacking them. Thread the eye pin through one of a gnome's hands so he is holding the bouquet. Bend the eye-pin wire back around to the front of the gnome's hand using chain-nose pliers, and wrap the eye-pin wire around the base of the bouquet to secure it. Repeat for both of each gnome's hands.

WHISTLE AT WORK *earrings*

Even when they're riding their deer into work and get stuck in a traffic jam, gnomes are still whistling and happy as clams. These deer earrings pay tribute to the gnome-preferred form of transportation.

63

Who says watches are just for your wrists? Watch faces are easy to find at thrift stores and flea markets, and they're just begging to be transformed into something new and fun. Even if the watch no longer works, it will make your locks look lovely. More important, it will remind you every time you check your 'do in the mirror that quitting time is never far away. I suggest setting the watch to five o'clock so it's perpetually quitting time—not only in your head, but on your head as well.

QUITTING TIME
headband

skill level:
FIRST DAY ON THE JOB

TAKE A MEMO

While I was a Naughty Secretary, I also was a business-savvy entrepreneur planning my world takeover in between taking messages. This entailed a lot of time on the Internet searching for inspiration, swapping Web site links with like-minded crafters and chatting with other indie business people. Here are a few of my favorite online haunts:

Etsy: www.etsy.com
Etsy is like a twenty-four-hour, constantly changing, worldwide craft bazaar. Buy and sell handmade goods all the day long.

Craftster: www.craftster.org
Have a question about why your resin bracelet has bubbles or what is the best embroidery stitch to use? Craftster is where you go to ask like-minded crafters your burning questions, as well as to show off your finished projects.

The Switchboards: www.theswitchboards.com
Think your handmade jewelry is good enough to start selling on Etsy or your own Web site? Go to the Switchboards to ask for business advice.

Flickr: www.flickr.com
Flickr is an online picture-sharing community, but not just for vacation pictures. You can add contacts so you can see others' photos and join pools about jewelry and crafts to show off projects.

Continued on page 67...

STUFF YOU'LL NEED

wide plastic headband

leopard-print craft felt

sheer red ribbon

green grosgrain ribbon (narrower than the red ribbon)

watch face

clothespins

fabric glue

scissors

chain-nose pliers

1 GATHER MATERIALS

Round up all your materials, including a piece of leopard-print craft felt, 2 kinds of ribbon (1 narrower than the other, for layering), a wide plastic headband, an old watch, fabric glue, scissors, chain-nose pliers and some clothespins.

2 MEASURE AND CUT FELT

Place the headband on the felt diagonally so that the felt reaches all the way around the headband. Cut the felt so there's enough to cover the entire headband and wrap around nicely to the underside.

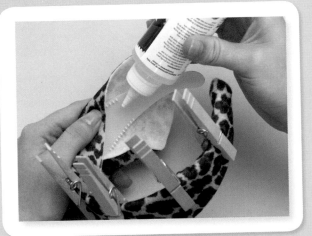

3 ADHERE FELT TO HEADBAND

Wrap the cut felt around the headband, securing it on the underside of the headband with fabric glue and pinning it in place as you go with clothespins.

4 REMOVE WATCH FACE FROM BAND

Use chain-nose pliers to remove the watch face from the watchband.

MEMO CONTINUED...

Beading Daily: www.beadingdaily.com
Just as the name implies, if you want a daily dose of beading inspiration, this is the place for you.

SuperNaturale: www.supernaturale.com
This is another large message board for crafters. However, SuperNaturale also has informative articles and advice columns.

Austin Craft Mafia: www.austincraftmafia.com
The original craft mafia was started in Austin by me and a few of my crafty friends. Our site has some great business resources as well as informative interviews with the founding members.

getcrafty: www.getcrafty.com
When your crafty wheels are turning and five o'clock is a long way away, you will be thankful for yet another online craft community.

5 ADHERE FIRST RIBBON TO HEADBAND, THREAD ON WATCH FACE

Beginning on the underside of the headband, adhere the red ribbon in the center of the leopard-print craft felt with fabric glue. Wrap the ribbon around the end of the headband, then up and over the top of the band and around to the under side again. Be sure not to get too crazy with the glue. If you use too much, the glue will soak through your ribbon and leave dark spots. Secure the ribbon with clothespins and allow the glue to dry. Thread the watch face onto a length of the grosgrain ribbon. Repeat on the other side of the watch face with a second length of grosgrain ribbon.

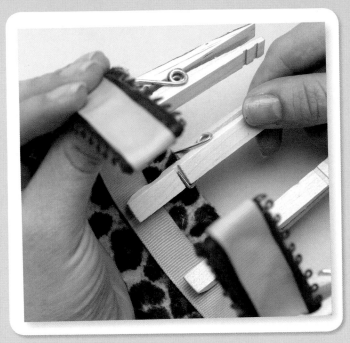

6 ADHERE WATCH FACE AND RiBBON TO HEADBAND

Position the watch face slightly off center on the top of the headband and wrap the ribbon around to the underside of the headband as with the first ribbon. Adhere the ribbon with fabric glue directly in the center of the red ribbon, leaving a slim border of red on either side of the green ribbon.

7 SECURE RiBBONS WiTH CLOTHESPiNS

Secure the ribbons with clothespins and allow the glue to dry fully. Remove the clothespins when the glue is set.

TIE ONE ON
headbands

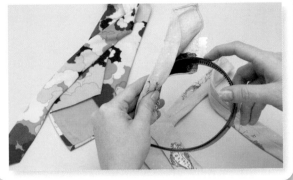

Here's the lunchtime game plan:
Vintage man's necktie? Check.
Cheap drugstore headband? Check.
Two minutes of your time? Check.
Looks like you have everything you need to whip up
some hair-control hotness. Your boss will be so proud.

In case you haven't noticed, ties are basically fabric tubes with one end larger than the other. So there's no need to sew or glue for this project. Starting at the fat end of the tie, guide the headband all the way into the tie. Center the headband so the tie tails fall evenly. Now slip on the headband and tie the tie's tails at the nape of your neck as you would when tying a scarf around your head. Instantly you will have the look of a businesswoman on her way to the top.

Make as many of these easy tie-covered headbands as your little heart desires. Raid the thrift store for ties, match them up to skinny or fat plastic headbands, depending on the tie's width, and get crazy making a headband for everyone you know.

69

TRANSFER ME
jewelry

If you can't beat 'em, join 'em. I figure if the scrapbooking trend is going to take up half of the craft store, I might as well start perusing the aisle looking for jewelry-making goodies. Here I made a few office-appropriate bangles using rub-ons with hidden stealth messages for coworkers, such as "You're My Type" for that cutie in legal, "I'm the Boss" for when I start to doubt myself, and pictures of robots for when one person too many treats me like a machine.

What's a pirate's favorite letter? RRrrrrrrrrr...

1 RUB ON DESIGN

Cut around the rub-on(s) you would like to use for your design. Spend a bit of time planning out your design, making sure everything fits and arranging the rub-ons how you'd like them to go. Then position each rub-on at the spot where you want it, ink side down, and burnish the back with a craft stick. Make sure to rub the entire design evenly and with firm pressure.

2 REMOVE PROTECTIVE BACKING

Peel back a bit of the carrier plastic to make sure the design is transferring as it should. If not, replace the plastic and continue to burnish. If the design has transferred, lift away the clear carrier plastic. If you'd like, you can paint over the entire bracelet with découpage medium, or spray it with a clear sealant to protect the transfer.

TRANSFER ME *pendants*

Rub ons come in all shapes and sizes, including adorable owl images, skulls and fancy script letters.

These handy-dandy rub-on transfers clearly are not limited to just the pages of a scrapbook. Keep your eyeballs peeled for plain plastic jewelry to adorn with rub-ons, such as these vintage cameo pendants I found.

71

These sassy little secretaries desperately want to think outside the box, but since they are permanently suspended inside resin cubes, that is a bit of a challenge. The techniques used to make this bracelet are actually quite easy. Once you get the hang of it, you, too, will be thinking outside the resin box and floating everything from miniature toys to pictures of your grandma in the resin.

SECRETARY'S DELIGHT
bracelet & ring set

START HERE

skill level:
RUNNING THE SHOW

BABIES AND PILLS
bracelet

One of the few bonuses of working for the man is having health insurance, which makes getting things like prescriptions and maternity leave a little bit easier. This is a bracelet to celebrate that perk.

STUFF YOU'LL NEED

images for bracelet and ring (see page 137) or anything else you'd like to suspend inside resin cubes

photograph-quality printer paper

clear casting resin

catalyst

glitter

9 10.5mm silver-tone jump rings

ring blank

lobster clasp

dedicated clear plastic cups for mixing resin

ice cube tray

scissors

craft stick

clear topcoat spray paint

high-speed drill with sanding attachment and larger bit

computer printer

scanner

chain-nose pliers

73

1 PREPARE IMAGES

Scan the sassy secretary images on page 137 into your computer. Use a photo program to make the images ⁹⁄₁₀" (2cm) wide by 1³⁄₁₀" (3cm) tall and 300 dpi. Print the images on heavy photo-quality paper. (Resin will soak through text-weight paper and turn it dark.) Cut out the 6 images, beveling (or rounding) the corners of each picture.

2 POUR RESIN AND CATALYST

Follow the manufacturer's instructions for the ratio of resin to catalyst, and then pour the 2 substances into a plastic cup (don't use Styrofoam—the resin will eat through it). Since resin sets up and hardens quickly, you will have to mix a new very small batch for every layer. HINT: I find that going a little heavy on the catalyst helps your resin set up and dry better. Don't go too heavy, though—it also will make your resin more brittle.

3 MIX RESIN AND CATALYST

Use a craft stick to mix the resin and catalyst together. Don't worry about the bubbles—those are supposed to be there.

4 POUR RESIN

Making resin jewelry entails pouring many thin layers. First, you want to pour a very thin layer into the bottom of 6 compartments in your ice cube tray. Let the resin set up for about 15 minutes, or until it begins to congeal and harden.

5 EMBED IMAGES IN RESIN CUBES

Mix another small batch of resin. Pour another thin layer on top of the first slightly hard layer. Into this wet layer of resin, lay each image square into the ice cube tray, image side down (remember, you are making your cubes upside down). Gently push on each image with a craft stick or straw, forcing the bubbles in the resin up around the sides of the image. Make sure you pour enough resin so that it is coming around and just slightly covering the backside of each image.

6 ADD GLITTER

Sprinkle glitter onto the surface of each resin cube. Mix a larger batch of resin and fill up 6 of the ice cube tray compartments to about ¼" (6mm) from the top. (5 cubes will be for the bracelet, and 1 is for the ring.) You will just have to eyeball this step. How much resin you pour is also contingent on how thick your previous layers were. How fat you want your cubes to be is up to you.

TAKE A MEMO

Pantyhose to the rescue! Just because your pantyhose have a run doesn't mean they've lost their usefulness. Oh no, pantyhose have a second career as one of the most useful items in your home, ranking right up there with safety pins and the microwave. Here are just a few things pantyhose can do, even with a run.

- *Polish your furniture:* Assuming you own furniture worth polishing, rub it with polish applied to wadded-up pantyhose.
- *Tie up droopy houseplants:* If your houseplant is starting to flop, tie it to a stake with a strip of pantyhose.
- *Find lost jewels:* Did your heirloom pearls break and roll under the bookcase? Cut a piece of pantyhose and secure it with a rubber band around the end of your vacuum cleaner hose. Turn on the vacuum cleaner, snake the hose under the furniture, and voilà! Your pearls will be sucked against the pantyhose without being pulled into the vacuum cleaner bag.
- *Hold wrapping paper:* Keep your half-used rolls of wrapping paper or wallpaper wrinkle free by storing them in a pantyhose leg. If you have a lot, put some in each leg then store them by hanging the pantyhose over your closet pole.
- *Make a strainer:* Got lumpy paint? Just stretch some pantyhose material over the top and pour the paint through and into another container. No more lumps.
- *Make elastic bands:* Cut the waistband off pantyhose and use it to hold a trash bag in place around a trash can or to keep a sleeping bag or blanket neatly rolled.
- *Make a scrubber:* Cut off the foot, slip it over a sponge and tie off the end. You now have a great no-scratch scrubber for your pots, pans, sinks and whatever else needs scrubbing.
- *Recycle soap slivers:* Cut off a pantyhose leg and use it as a sack to hold those little slivers of soap you can't bring yourself to throw away but really can't use anymore. Once you've collected a little bundle, tie off the end of the pantyhose and use your "toe o' soap" like you would soap on a rope.

7 ADD RING BACK

Add your ring blank to the back side of one of the glitter-covered resin cubes. Sprinkle on a bit more glitter coating to cover the glue pad on your adjustable ring. Add your final layer of resin to thicken the cube as explained in step 6.

8 POP OUT RESIN CUBES AND RING

Allow the resin to harden and set up fully overnight. Then simply pop all of the resin cubes out of the tray. Your ring is basically finished, and the other cubes are ready to be drilled and used to create a bracelet.

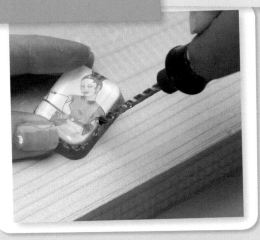

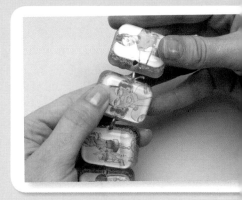

9 SAND BACKS OF CUBES

Use the high-speed drill with the sanding attachment to smooth the backs of all the resin cubes and to smooth the back of the ring. (See page 20 for instructions on sanding with a high-speed drill.)

10 DRiLL HOLES iN CUBES

Use the high-speed drill with the larger bit to drill a hole diagonally through the midpoint on each long side of each cube, from front to back. (See page 21 for instructions on drilling with a high-speed drill.) After all your pieces are drilled and sanded, take the cubes outside and spray them with a clear shiny topcoat. If you used a brand-spanking-new ice cube tray, your cubes should be shiny enough already, but the backsides still will need to be topcoated because they may be tacky from the resin. Allow the topcoat to dry thoroughly.

11 CONSTRUCT BRACELET

Open a jump ring and slide it through one of the holes in one of the cubes. Slide the next cube onto the open jump ring, and then close it. Continue linking the cubes in this manner until you have fashioned an entire bracelet. Add a chain of 2 jump rings to the final jump ring on one side of the bracelet. Slide a lobster clasp onto a jump ring and link it to the final jump ring on the other side of the bracelet. (See page 19 for instructions on opening and closing a jump ring.)

HOT TIP

Drilling a hole through resin at an angle ensures that the hole will be sturdy and still narrow enough so a jump ring can link two cubes together. If you're a beginner, you might want to fill the whole ice cube tray with resin so that if you mess up, you have a back-up handy.

Beaded collars are not readily available these days, so I created my own customizable version. Back in the day, ladies often wore frilly little blouses with large Peter Pan collars. Then along came Lana Turner, who made tailored sweater sets fashionable. A pencil skirt and dark pumps finished the look. Ladies loved the new look, but they still longed for those Peter Pan collars. Some crafty jewelry designer filled the void by designing a detachable beaded collar. This collar, usually made with faux pearls, could be worn with a sweater set to spice up the outfit. It became a staple in the wardrobe of every woman in the 1950s. With its secret message, this Pink Collar is a throwback to the original beaded collar. I chose to write "This Job Sucks," but if you heart your job, you could write that instead.

PiNK *collar*

SIGN HERE

FLOWER *combs*

Here's another favorite throwback hair accessory. You may not see many of these around today, but they're still pretty and still functional. You can't very well be voted employee of the month if you are trying to work with hair in your face! Customize a comb for your lovely locks with charms and plastic flower petals.

STUFF YOU'LL NEED

1 sheet of interfacing

1 piece of white felt

1 yd (91cm) strand of pink fancy pearl edging*

1 yd (91cm) 1/4" (7mm) wide fancy pearl edging for border*

6 yds (5.5m) strand of white fancy pearl edging*

skinny round white elastic

button-covering kit

small piece of white fabric (for covering button)

white sewing thread and needle

clothespins

pen or pencil (optional)

fabric glue

scissors

iron

* all of the pearls are sold as attached strands and are available by the yard in fabric stores

79

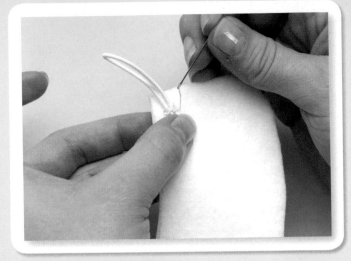

1 FUSE INTERFACING TO COLLAR AND CUT OUT

Use an iron to fuse a piece of interfacing to a piece of white felt. Cut out the collar using the template on page 136. Peel the paper backing off the piece of interfacing.

2 SEW ON BUTTON LOOP

Cut a 1½" (4cm) length of skinny round white elastic and bend it in half. Use a sewing needle and thread to secure the ends of the doubled-over elastic to one end of the collar to create a button loop.

3 COVER BUTTON AND SEW ONTO COLLAR

Use the button-covering kit to cover a button with white fabric. Glue pink fancy pearl edging onto the button in a spiral shape with fabric glue so the entire button is covered. Move the pearl edging around as little as possible, as it can bleed once it's been in contact with the glue. Allow the glue to dry. Sew the button onto the end of the collar opposite the button loop with a sewing needle and white thread.

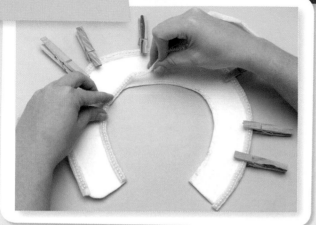

⁴ ADHERE PEARL EDGING TO COLLAR

Glue the fancy pearl edging around the perimeter of the collar with fabric glue. Clip the pearl edging in place with clothespins along the curved edge of the collar as it dries.

⁵ OUTLINE PHRASE WITH PINK PEARLS

Using your computer, write "This Job Sucks" or the phrase of your choice in a script font. Experiment with the size until you are sure it will fit onto the collar. Using the printed words as a guide to the size and shape, lightly write the words onto the collar with a pencil or an ink pen that doesn't bleed when wet. Allow the glue to dry.

⁶ FILL IN REMAINING SPACE WITH WHITE FANCY PEARL EDGING

Use fabric glue to adhere white fancy pearl edging around the words, filling any empty space. Zigzag the edging back and forth between the borders and around the words. Allow the glue to dry.

TAKE A MEMO

We have all heard of White Collar jobs and Blue Collar jobs, but there is also another category, Pink Collar jobs. Never heard of it? Unlike Blue Collar jobs, which generally require sweating, or White Collar jobs, which require bossing people around, Pink Collar jobs are relatively clean, don't require heavy lifting and are traditionally female. All three terms are fairly antique, and you don't hear them often.

I won't bore you with a long history of how women began entering the workforce during the Industrial Revolution or how they were kept out of better-paying jobs due to prejudice or physical requirements. I do want to point out, however, that as of 2007, only twelve women were CEOs of *Fortune* 500 companies. We've come a long way, baby, but we still have a long way to go.

Everyone who has ever had a job she despised (and who hasn't?) has watched the clock ticking down the minutes until quitting time. Why just watch the clock when you could be making it into jewelry and wearing it? Set all the clocks in your jewelry to five o'clock to help you remember that quitting time always comes around sooner or later.

CLOCK WATCHER *necklace*

skill level:
YOU DESERVE A RAISE

TAKE A MEMO

Did you know Dolly Parton came up with the beat for "9 to 5" while tapping her long nails? (Perhaps something you do as you watch the minutes before five o'clock slowly tick by?) Did you know White Out (Liquid Paper) was invented by Bette Nesmith Graham, a.k.a. the mother of Mike Nesmith of The Monkees fame? If you are at work and bored to tears, make sure you have a bottle of white correction fluid handy. Oh, and a permanent marker, too. Keep in mind, correction fluid and permanent markers aren't really meant to be used on your nails—so decorate your fingertips at your own risk!

French Manicure: Place a piece of clear tape across your fingernail, leaving just the part of the nail that rises above your fingertip visible. Use brush-on white correction fluid to paint the tips of your nails white. When the correction fluid is dry, gently remove the tape to reveal your French manicure. Repeat for your toenails.

Domino Nails: Color all your nails with a black permanent marker, applying multiple coats if necessary. When the marker is dry, Google "domino" on the computer at your desk, and use the online pictures as a guide. Use a white correction fluid pen to draw a horizontal line across the center of each nail. Then get polka-dot crazy, making each nail a domino replica.

Polka-Dot Nails: Use brush-on or pen correction fluid to make dots on your nails. This looks best atop red fingernails.

STUFF YOU'LL NEED

gold-tone vintage secretary badge

2 gold-tone "hours worked" decorative plates

4 gold-tone tassels

30 4mm gold-tone jump rings

6 watch faces

6 gold-tone rectangular plates

8¹/₂" (22cm) gold-tone linked chain

chain-nose pliers

wire cutters

83

1 BEGIN TO ASSEMBLE PENDANT

Use chain-nose pliers to take apart the vintage secretary badge. Link the 2 "hours worked" decorative plates to the secretary piece with jump rings. (See page 19 for instructions on opening and closing a jump ring.) Since these pieces are vintage, you will be hard-pressed to find the exact pieces shown here. So just substitute anything you might have on hand to make the centerpiece of your necklace.

2 FINISH ASSEMBLING PENDANT

Open the top loop of each gold-tone tassel and link 1 to the bottom loops of each "hours worked" plate.

3 REMOVE WATCH FACES FROM BANDS

Use wire cutters to remove the faces from 6 vintage ladies' watches. Be sure to select 6 that have a single vertical loop on the top and 1 loop on the bottom for easy linking.

4 LINK WATCH FACES AND PLATES

The gold-tone rectangular plates are salvaged from a vintage necklace. You could use any other gold-colored plates you like. Start by attaching 2 jump rings to each end of your plate. Then link a watch face to a plate. Continue linking watch faces and gold plates until your chain is the desired length. Repeat for the other side. Attach a closure to the ends of your chain.

6 ADD CHAIN TO FINISH NECKLACE

Link each end of an 8¾" (22cm) gold-tone linked chain to the 2 end gold-tone plates with jump rings.

5 LINK WATCH-FACE CHAIN TO PENDANT

Link each watch-face chain to the top of the pendant with a jump ring.

CLOCK WATCHER
earrings and bracelet

Make a simple wrapped loop to link watch faces to earring wires. Add tassels for some sassy secretarial swing.

Did you know the wristwatch is becoming extinct? Everyone carries a cell phone with a clock these days, so wristwatches are becoming obsolete. In the future, men probably will be the only people wearing watches, only because a wristwatch is one of the few pieces of jewelry they can get away with wearing. I personally find that so, so sad. But I digress. Even if women some day cease to wear timepieces, the wristwatch bracelet will never go out of style.

Once in a great while you'll find a unique piece that makes a perfect pendant. You'll wish you could make twenty copies, but you can't, of course. Well, sometimes wishes do come true, and a Melting Pot can make it happen. You can make as many "copies" of your pendant, charm or knickknack as you like in just about any color under the rainbow. However, I would not recommend sitting on this copy machine in a skirt.

COPY MACHINE *necklace*

SIGN HERE

skill level:
YOU DESERVE A RAISE

NAMEPLATE *necklace*

A necklace that spells out who you are is so much cuter than a "Hello My Name Is" tag.

TAKE A MEMO

Take note that in the movie *9 to 5* both Doralee and Violet wear nameplate necklaces. Use individual letter stamps and the same Copy Machine Necklace supplies to make your own personalized necklace.

STUFF YOU'LL NEED

2-part mix for molding material (Mold-n-Pour)

colored ultra-thick embossing enamel in powdered form (UTEE)

UTEE flex crystals

charms and trinkets to use for molds

jump ring

Melting Pot

high-speed drill with small bit

disposable stirring stick

chain-nose pliers

1 CHOOSE OBJECT FOR MOLDING

Choose an object with a smooth surface and with a design that is not too terribly intricate with which to make your mold. It should be something that will leave a strong, clear impression in the molding material.

2 MIX 2-PART MOLDING AGENT

Mix equal parts of the 2-part molding agent together in your hands.

3 MAKE MOLD

Shape the mixed molding agent into a rough ball and flatten it out on your work surface into a small pancake shape. Press the object you've chosen face down into the molding agent. Hold the object there with firm pressure for about 1 minute while the mold sets.

4 REMOVE CHARM FROM MOLD

Remove the object from the molding agent, revealing the finished mold.

5 POUR iN UTEE POWDER AND MELT

Follow the manufacturer's instructions for heating up the UTEE in the Melting Pot. The hotter the UTEE, the faster it flows when you pour, so melt it thoroughly and cool it slightly for a more steady pour into your mold.

6 MiX iN FLEX

Add some flex to the melted UTEE. Allow 1 scoop of flex for every 4 scoops of UTEE. Mix the substances together with a disposable stirring stick to blend them thoroughly.

HOT TIP

If your finished object comes out badly, with bubbles or other imperfections, you can just put it right back in the Melting Pot and start over.

7 POUR MiXTURE iNTO MOLD

Pour the mixture in the Melting Pot into the mold. Allow the mixture to rest for about 2 minutes, or until it's cool to the touch. Tap the back of your poured pendant to make sure it has cooled and hardened.

8 REMOVE FiNiSHED CHARM FROM MOLD

Pop the charm out of the mold. Drill a hole at the top of the charm, if desired. Link the pendant to a length of chain with a jump ring to make a necklace.

HELLO MY NAME IS

Dottie D.

How may I help you today?

There are some offices where you can just waltz right in the front door. There are others, however, that take their cue from the CIA. There is a metal detector and a security guard —usually an elderly man who didn't want to spend his golden years watching soaps with his wife. These bastions of safety inevitably require a name badge. There is no reason why your name badge has to stay in the same sterile state in which human resources gave it to you. Trick that badge out and make everyone else in the office covet your customized all-access pass.

ALL-ACCESS PASS
badge holder

skill level:
YOU DESERVE A RAISE

STUFF YOU'LL NEED

1 sheet ink-jet-safe printer fabric

craft felt

orange embroidery floss

rectractable badge or pen holder

polyester fiberfill

pin back

scanner

computer

ink-jet printer

scissors

embroidery needle

1 CUT OUT FRONT AND BACK OF BADGE HOLDER

Scan a secretary image provided on page 91 into your computer at a high resolution. Tweak the image on your computer to make the picture about 3" to 4" (8cm to 10cm) tall and 300 dpi for high print quality. Print the image onto a piece of printer fabric following the manufacturer's instructions. Loosely cut around the image and place it atop your craft felt. Cut out the exact outline of the secretary shape.

2 SEW BADGE FRONT AND BACK TOGETHER

With orange embroidery floss and an embroidery needle, whipstitch around the edges of the 2 fabric pieces to join the front and back of the badge holder. Leave the bottom of the badge holder partially open.

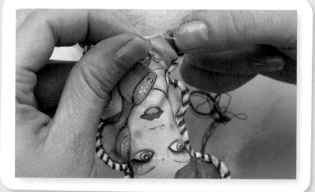

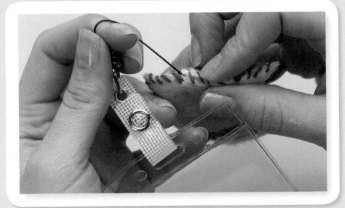

3 STUFF BADGE HOLDER

Stuff the badge holder with polyester fiberfill through the opening at the bottom of the badge holder.

4 INSERT RETRACTABLE DEVICE INTO BADGE HOLDER

Insert the retractable device into the bottom of the badge holder and whipstitch around it, securing it inside the badge holder.

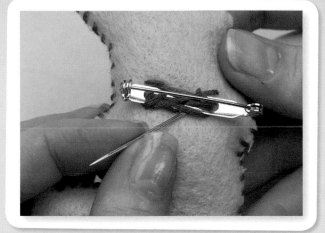

5 SEW ON PiN BACK

Use embroidery floss and an embroidery needle to sew the pin back to the back of the badge holder.

ANOTHER *badge holder*

Use any image you like to create a customized pillowy badge holder. Substitute pens and pencils on your trusty yet fashionable retractable badge holder.

TAKE A MEMO

Two types of embroidery stitches were used to edge these stuffed fabric badge holders. Both are particularly good for finishing fabric edges and preventing fraying.

The simplest of all hand stitches is the whipstitch. This straight, angled stitch partially covers the top edges of the front and back of the fabric, providing a more finished edge. The closer the stitches, the more of the edge is covered.

For this project, begin the stitch approximately 1/8" (3mm) below the fabric edge. Insert the needle from back to front. Bring the needle over the edge and reinsert it from back to front approximately 1/8" (3mm) from the first stitch. Continue stitching all the way around the badge. Don't pull the thread so tight that the edge of the fabric curls over. Just use firm, even tension.

The second stitch I used is the blanket stitch. As the name implies, it's traditionally used to finish the edges of blankets.

Begin by securing the floss with a tiny stitch on the backside of the piece. (I also knotted the end of the floss, although there is debate about whether to use a knot. Or not. For the purposes of this little project, the knot debate falls under the category of "Way Too Much Information.") With the front facing you, bring the needle around to the front and insert it approximately 1/8" (3mm) below the edge and approximately 1/8" (3mm) over from that first tiny stitch. Pull it through to the back, leaving a slight loop in the floss. Bring the needle back up through that loop and pull the loop tight. Repeat this process by inserting the needle approximately 1/8" (3mm) over from the first stitch. Bring it back up and through the loop made by this stitch. Continue stitching all the way around the piece. Finish by securing the thread with a tiny stitch or two on the back.

Let me finish this little tutorial by admitting I am a visual learner when it comes to any kind of handwork. If reading this doesn't make sense to you, there are plenty of clear, easily understood diagrams for both of these stitches on the Internet.

Do you ever feel as if you are literally tied to your job? I know the feeling. In response, I have designed the Tied Down Brooch. Take that symbol of masculine authority, the tie, and cut it down to size. Turn the concept of male-as-boss upside down, and you'll end up with one sassy accessory that will make you the belle of the office ball.

TiED DOWN *brooch*

TAKE A MEMO

These amazingly awesome administrative assistants didn't let any tie-wearing male boss stand in their way.

Doralee Rhodes (played by Dolly Parton in *9 to 5*)

Jennifer Elizabeth Marlowe (played by Loni Anderson on *WKRP in Cincinnati*)

Lee Holloway (played by Maggie Gyllenhaal in *Secretary*)

Tess McGill (played by Melanie Griffith in *Working Girl*)

Selina Kyle/Catwoman (played by Michelle Pfeiffer in *Batman Returns*)

Judy Bernly (played by Jane Fonda in *9 to 5*)

Violet Newstead (played by Lily Tomlin in *9 to 5*)

Guy (played by Frank Whaley in *Swimming with Sharks*)

Andy Sachs (played by Anne Hathaway in *The Devil Wears Prada*)

Amanda Tanen (played by Becki Newton in *Ugly Betty*)

BOWTiE COMBS *and necklace*

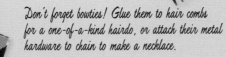

Don't forget bowties! Glue them to hair combs for a one-of-a-kind hairdo, or attach their metal hardware to chain to make a necklace.

skill level:
RUNNING THE SHOW

STUFF YOU'LL NEED

3 or 4 ties in a color scheme of your choice

cotton batting

interfacing

pin back

button-covering kit

sewing machine and thread

sewing needle and thread

fabric glue

straight pins

scissors

iron

95

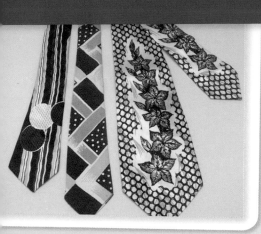

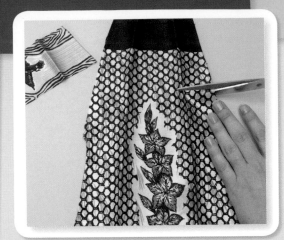

1 CHOOSE TiES

Pick out 3 coordinating ties and lay them out together.

2 CUT OUT RECTANGLES

Cut up the backs of the ties to open up the fabric. Cut 9 rectangles out of the widest part of the ties. (Each rectangle should be twice as wide as it is tall so it makes a square when folded in step 3.)

3 SEW SQUARES

With right sides together, fold each rectangle in half to make a square. Sew along one of the edges adjacent to the fold. Repeat for all 9 rectangles.

4 TRiM TRiANGLES

Turn each sewn square right-side out, and trim along the open edge to form a triangle. Repeat for all 9 squares. Iron each triangle.

5 PiN AND SEW TRiANGLES

Lay out all the triangles in a straight line in an order you like. Overlap the triangles slightly and pin them together. Sew along the straight edge of the overlapping triangles with a basting stitch set to a long stitch length, the longest one on your machine.

6 PULL THREAD TO CREATE CiRCLE

Tug at the thread tails until the 9-triangle banner curls up on itself to create a circle. This can be slow going. Just be patient, pull a little on the thread, then push th wrinkled fabric, taking care not to break the thread.

7 SECURE BROOCH SHAPE

Cut out a circle of cotton batting about 2½" (7cm) in diameter. Manipulate the crinkled-up triangles into a 2-layer circle. Pin the 2-layer circle to the felt circle. Handstitch the double-layer circle of petals to the felt circle.

8 CUT TiE TAiLS AND SEW ON TO BROOCH

Cut 2 tie tails to approximately 11" (28cm) and sew them to the back of the brooch, overlapping them slightly.

9 COVER BUTTON FOR BROOCH CENTER

Cut out a small square of tie fabric and put it right-side down into the plastic cup of the button-covering kit. Slide the button back into the plastic cup and then push down hard with the blue cup to secure the button cover.

10 ADHERE BUTTON

Position the button on the center of the brooch, in the center of the 2 layers of petals. Glue the button on with fabric glue.

11 COVER BROOCH BACK WiTH FABRiC CiRCLE

Cut out a circle of tie fabric to fit the back of the brooch and cover up the messy stitches. Iron a circle of interfacing onto the back of the tie fabric. Sew it in place with a needle and thread. Attach the pin back with fabric glue.

As a child, were you the one who could not be torn away from your toy typewriter, laying the groundwork for a career that was years ahead of you? Well, just because you are typing on a big girl typewriter these days—oh wait, scratch that, I mean computer—does not mean you have to give up your favorite childhood toy.

TiN TYPEWRITER *bracelet*

skill level:
RUNNING THE SHOW

✩ ✩ ✩

TAKE A MEMO

Typewriters and toys are not the only metal pieces you can use for jewelry. Remember the great graphics on those decorative tins Grandma used for sending you cookies? Have you ever stumbled upon an old coffee can at a thrift store that made your toes curl in delight? Have you been to an Asian grocery store lately? Any thin-walled metal object will work for these projects in much the same way as the tin typewriter I used to make this bracelet. The key is to start training yourself to look at everything—even food containers—as a possible piece of jewelry.

Metal containers are usually a good choice because they have thin walls and are relatively easy to cut. (Not to put too fine a point on it, but while we still refer to cans as "tin cans," generally tin is no longer used for containers. Now they're usually made from aluminum.) Use your metal cutters to snip out the images, such flowers from a cookie tin or silhouettes of coffee drinkers on a coffee can. File the edges smooth as you did for the bracelet. Use your awl and eyelets to transform that image into a pendant. Hang it from a piece of chain and you're done!

STUFF YOU'LL NEED

old toy tin typewriter

jump rings

black eyelets

lobster clasp

metal cutters

hammer

rubber mallet

eyelet setter

awl

small craft mat

small metal files

bastard file

ball-peen hammer

chain-nose pliers

round-nose pliers

1 GATHER MATERIALS AND TOOLS

Gather all the materials and tools you'll need to make this bracelet, including an old toy tin typewriter and metal cutters.

2 REMOVE KEYBOARD FROM TOY TYPEWRITER

They don't make toys like they used to, so needless to say it takes a little elbow grease to get these parts separated. A set of pliers (not the jewelry kind) might come in handy here.

3 CUT KEYBOARD INTO RECTANGULAR PIECES

Once you have your keyboard cut out, decide what size you would like the sections of your bracelet to be. Use metal cutters to cut out 4 equal-sized rectangles. Mine are 2" (5cm) wide by 1½" (4cm) tall.

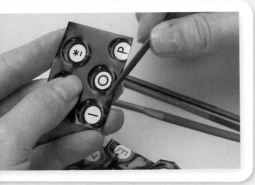

4 SAND METAL PIECES

Starting with a bastard file, sand the rough edges of your 4 tin pieces. Be careful not to poke yourself and also not to chip the paint on the keyboard. Follow up the bastard file with smaller metal files until the edges of each section are smooth to the touch.

5 TURN CORNERS UNDER

Use round-nose pliers to curl the sharp corners of each bracelet section around to the back of the tin piece. After you have turned all 4 corners under, gently tap the corners with your rubber mallet to flatten them.

6 SET EYELETS

Use your awl to start the holes on your bracelet links, making sure they're smaller than your eyelets. Set 3 links with eyelets in all 4 corners. For the final link, set 2 holes on one side and a single center hole on the other. Insert an eyelet into one of the holes from front to back. Lay the tin piece face down on a small craft mat. Place the eyelet setter over the eyelet and hit the eyelet setter with a ball-peen hammer to flatten the back of the eyelet, setting it in place. Repeat for the remaining holes in all the sections.

7 LINK BRACELET PIECES TOGETHER

Link the bracelet sections together with jump rings. On the end of the bracelet with 2 holes, make a chain of 2 jump rings for each hole, and then connect the 2 chains with 1 more jump ring. Link the clasp to this connecting jump ring with 1 slightly smaller jump ring. Finish the other end of the bracelet with a chain of 2 jump rings. (See page 19 for instructions on opening and closing jump rings.)

TYPEWRITER *belt buckle*

STUFF YOU'LL NEED

center dial of old toy tin typewriter

belt buckle blank

E-6000 adhesive

Vintage tin typewriters are too cute not to use up every part. Make a super easy and unique belt buckle out of the leftover scraps.

Gather all your materials. Then adhere the tin dial to the belt buckle blank of your choice with E-6000. Allow it to dry. Snap it into place on the belt. Wear with pride.

TGiF

Friday is that magical day we live for all week long. Besides the fact that your workweek is over and you are energized about the weekend ahead, there are a few other magical events that happen on this particular day of the week. Two sets of two words: happy hour (see page 104) and casual Friday (see page 108). Both of these events are immortalized in this chapter along with other hot Friday topics like business trips (see page 112). Friday is that day that makes you feel as if the weekend is your creative oyster and you have two whole days all to yourself to play with doll furniture and break little kids' glasses.

After a long, hard day at the office, nothing beats happy hour with coworkers. This gathering usually occurs at an establishment close to your place of employment and is spent taking advantage of discounted tasty beverages and slandering your employer's name. Even at the bar, the naughty secretary is on the prowl for jewelry supplies—no swizzle stick or cherry sword is left on the cocktail table when you are done.

HAPPY HOUR
charm bracelet

SIGN HERE

skill level:
YOU DESERVE A RAISE

SWIZZLE STICK
necklace

If your swizzle stick is large enough, it can be transformed into a pendant for a necklace.

STUFF YOU'LL NEED

5 vintage plastic swizzle sticks of your choice

6 plastic beech nut beads

12 yellow (or color of your choice to complement swizzle stick colors) E beads

approx. 7" (18cm) silver-tone link chain

13 oval jump rings

6 silver-tone head pins

1 silver-tone toggle clasp

high-speed drill with cutting attachment and small drill bit

chain-nose pliers

wire cutters

1 CUT OFF TOPS OF SWIZZLE STICKS

Use the high-speed drill with the cutting attachment to cut the decorative part off each swizzle stick. Drill a hole at the top of each piece using the high-speed drill and a small bit. (See page 21 for instructions on drilling with a high-speed drill.)

2 LINK SWIZZLE CHARMS AND BEADED HEAD PINS TO LINKED CHAIN

Slide a swizzle charm onto an oval jump ring and link it to the silver chain. (See page 19 for instructions on opening and closing a jump ring.) Slide a yellow E bead, a large beech nut bead and another yellow E bead onto a head pin and make a wrapped loop above the beads. (See page 18 for instructions on making a wrapped loop.) Slide the beaded head pin onto a jump ring and link the charm to the chain, approximately 2 links from the swizzle charm. Continue to link charms every 2 links, alternating between swizzle charms and beaded head pins. Link the bar end of the toggle clasp to one end of the bracelet with an oval jump ring. Link the circle end of the clasp to the other end of the chain with an oval jump ring.

HOT TIP

If your local watering hole does not have swizzle sticks, keep an eye peeled at flea markets and online. They are easy to find and come in oodles of fun shapes and sizes.

JUNK FOOD *jewelry*

I think fast food was invented for people who have an hour lunch break. Hit the miniatures aisle at your local craft store and whip yourself up some jewelry in homage.

FRENCH FRIES

Cola

How about some fries with that shake?

TAKE A MEMO

After five years as an administrative assistant, I learned to make a mean pot of coffee. Before this life experience, coffee filters were foreign things to me. I still don't drink coffee, but apparently I should buy filters because you can do a lot more with them than just make coffee.

· Have you ever had your cork break into your bottle of wine? You can't serve your friends a glass of Merlot with little bits of cork. Use a coffee filter to strain the wine.

· In the summer, you can never seem to eat a popsicle or ice cream cone fast enough without it melting and running down your arm. Poke your cone or popsicle stick through a coffee filter to act as a drip reservoir.

· Next time you are doing a little housecleaning, use a lint-free coffee filter to clean your windows and mirrors. Newspaper also works great!

· Once a year when you use your good china, restack it in the cabinet with a coffee filter between each plate for extra protection.

· It's hard to heat burritos and chili in the micro-wave without creating an explosion. Cover your grub with a coffee filter to prevent a big mess. Speaking of burritos, when yours is done use a new clean coffee filter to hold it. Works for hot dogs, too!

· Who needs cotton balls to remove toenail polish when you have perfectly good coffee filters on hand?

Everyone who has ever had an office job knows the beauty that is Casual Friday, that one special day of the week when you can leave your pantyhose at home and wear jeans and a T-shirt to the office. In the hands of a crafty Naughty Secretary, a T-shirt can be worn any day of the workweek. With a few snips and a quick dance with a sewing machine, your T-shirt will be transformed into a one-of-a-kind necklace that is completely "office appropriate."

CASUAL FRIDAY
T-shirt necklace

skill level:
RUNNING THE SHOW

SIGN HERE

I used my Naughty Secretary Club T-shirt because the design looks like a necklace. However, you can use any T-shirt with a fun image that tickles your fancy.

STUFF YOU'LL NEED

1 light blue Naughty Secretary Club T-shirt

lightweight quilt batting

fusible interfacing

red-and-white-polka-dotted cotton fabric

straight pins

sewing machine and red thread

scissors

iron

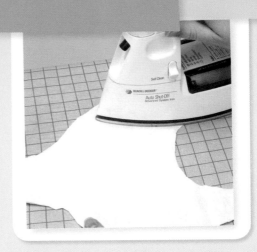

1 CUT NECKLACE DESIGN FROM T-SHIRT

Cut around the logo and wording on your T-shirt, starting by cutting down through both layers of the shirt at the shoulder. Open up the cutout and cut up to the shoulder seam in an arc back around to the other shoulder seam. Then cut out the collar to make it into a necklace shape large enough to accommodate your head.

2 IRON ON INTERFACING

Place the cutout T-shirt on top of a sheet of interfacing and cut the interfacing to the same size and shape as the T-shirt cutout. Iron the interfacing to the T-shirt.

3 PIN LAYERS TOGETHER

Layer the T-shirt cutout on top of a piece of red-and-white-polka-dotted fabric (wrong-side up) and a piece of white batting. Pin the layers together.

4 SEW LAYERS TOGETHER

Sew along the lines around the edges of the T-shirt cutout with red thread.

5 SEW AROUND BEADS

Sew around the beads to make them puff up and stand out.

6 CUT AROUND SEWN EDGES

Cut around the sewn edges of the necklace, cutting as close as you can without cutting the thread.

HOT TIP

If you want to make your beads extra puffy, you can add stuffing and make them really stand out. Turn the fabric to the back, cut a little hole in the backing fabric right beneath the area to stuff, then push in a little fiberfill. Handstitch the opening closed.

PAYDAY jewelry

Fridays are also paydays! With some faux money, jump rings, drill, chain and clasps, you can whip up some bling baubles quicker than it takes to deposit that check at the bank.

To make the coin necklace, drill 2 holes at opposite sides of each coin. (See page 21 for instructions on using a high-speed drill.) Link the coins together with jump rings. Link a chain of 2 jump rings to each end of the linked coins. Slide a lobster clasp on to one of the end jump rings. (See page 19 for instructions on opening and closing a jump ring.)

To make the bill necklace, drill holes in the top 2 corners of the plastic bill and link 1 piece of gold chain to the pendant with a jump ring. Repeat with a second length of gold chain. Add a clasp to the ends of the chain with jump rings.

HOTEL KEY
necklace

STUFF YOU'LL NEED

old hotel key chain

old key

vintage plastic flower beads

bead for flower center

18" (46cm) silver-tone linked chain with clasp

3" (8cm) silver-tone eye pin

6mm silver-tone jump ring

chain-nose pliers

wire cutters

skill level:
YOU DESERVE A RAISE

Traveling may be a hazard of the working world, but make the best of it! Next time you go to a conference, skip the fancy hotel. Maybe it does smell of fresh coffee and real flowers. And yes, it will have those comforting double safety locks on the door. But you'll be issued a generic credit-card-style room key. Naughty Secretary Club just hates that. Scout out a kitschy old hotel with a big neon vacancy. If you're lucky, they still will have the old-school room keys that just happen to make amazing souvenir necklaces. Now that's what traveling for business is all about.

Some people collect postcards and coins from their travels; others collect room keys.

1 SELECT MATERIALS

Choose an old abandoned hotel key chain or another small key, and then pick out several vintage plastic flower beads in a complementary color scheme. Choose a bead for the flower center, as well. Lay out all the pieces together to make sure you like the color scheme you've chosen.

2 SECURE STACKED FLOWERS TO KEY CHAIN

Slide the bead for the flower center onto an eye pin, then slide on all the plastic flowers, beginning with the smallest and ending with the largest. Slide the hotel key chain onto the eye pin. Use chain-nose pliers to bend the head pin straight up, flat against the back of the key chain. Bring the tail of the head pin back over the key chain and behind the flower petals, leaving a U shape of space at the top. Wrap and trim the tail of the wire neatly behind the flowers.

3 LINK KEY TO FLOWER CENTER

Link a key to the eye pin with a jump ring. (See page 19 for instructions on opening and closing a jump ring.) String the necklace chain through the U-shaped bail you created.

As the famous administrative professional's anthem goes: "Her pad is to write in, and not spend the night in." But no one said anything about making jewelry out of her furniture.

SECRETARY'S PAD *necklace*

skill level:
YOU DESERVE A RAISE

Visit garage sales and flea markets to find dollhouse furniture. Also let your friends with kids know you're keen for the tiny plastic items—they can hand them over once their kids are past the dollhouse stage. Another great way to find dollhouse furniture is to do an online search for miniatures.

STUFF YOU'LL NEED

1 piece of plastic dollhouse furniture

9 yellow-and-white-polka-dotted beads

10 yellow rectangular connector beads

1 silver-tone head pin

8 silver-tone eye pins

1 silver silhouette charm

11 small jump rings

20 small oval jump rings

1 hook-and-eye clasp

high-speed drill with small drill bit

chain-nose pliers

round-nose pliers

wire cutters

1 DRiLL HOLES iN PLASTiC FURNiTURE

Use the high-speed drill and a small bit to drill holes in each top corner of the dresser. Drill 1 hole through the center of the flat part of the dresser.

2 THREAD ON BEAD FOR CENTRAL DANGLE

Slide a head pin down through the hole you made in the center of the plastic piece of furniture. Slide a polka-dotted bead onto the head pin.

3 SECURE YELLOW BEAD UNDER DRESSER

Make a wrapped loop beneath the yellow bead using round-nose pliers. (See page 18 for instructions on making a wrapped loop.)

4 LiNK SiLHOUETTE CHARM TO YELLOW BEAD

Open a jump ring and slide the silver silhouette charm onto it. Link the jump ring to the loop beneath the yellow bead and close the jump ring. (See page 19 for instructions on opening and closing a jump ring.)

5 CREATE LINKED CHAIN

Slide a polka-dotted bead onto an eye pin and make a wrapped loop at the free end. Trim the excess wire with wire cutters. Repeat for each remaining polka-dotted bead. Link 1 polka-dotted bead to a yellow connector bead with a jump ring. Continue to make the chain, alternating between round beads and connector beads until you have linked 5 connectors and 4 polka-dotted beads, ending and beginning with a connector bead. Repeat to make a second chain.

6 ADD CLASP AND LINK CHAINS TO PENDANT

Link 1 clasp component to 1 end of each beaded chain. Link the remaining free ends of the chain to the 2 holes in the top of the dollhouse-furniture pendant with oval jump rings.

MORE SECRETARY'S PAD
jewelry

Any piece of furniture in your house (yup, including your toilet) comes in a miniature dollhouse size. Make necklaces, brooches, hair combs—the sky's the limit.

RED NECKLACE
variation

VANITY
hair comb

Gather your red and silver charms. If you are going to be making beads into charms for the tassel, do that first using a head pin and wire wrapping. When you have enough charms to fill all the strands of the tassels, take your small jump rings and start attaching. Feel free to use your wire cutters to trim the lengths of the tassels to even more arbitrary lengths. Once both tassels are filled with charms, drill 2 holes in the top part of the dresser.

Attach the chain to the eye pins. Thread the pins through the holes and wire-wrap them to secure. Attach tassels with jump rings.

GREEN SOFA + BLUE DRESSER *necklaces*

TAKE A MEMO

Why not decorate your secretary's pad with office supplies? Back in prehistoric office days before there were self-inking stamps, office workers everywhere kept an array of wooden stamps that required a separate ink pad on their desks. These stamps were for repetitive paperwork statements like "Important" and "Rejected." These old-fashioned long-necked rubber stamps lived in a metal home, called a stamp carousel, during their off time.

Nowadays, these types of stamps, as well as their holders, are a bit antiquated—that is until you think about what else they might be able to hold. These handy little displays are great for storing your bracelets. Each long metal prong can hold several bracelets, and the best part is that the carousel spins for easy access. Look for carousels at flea markets and places like ebay. I found mine at a used-office-supply store. You might not find stamp carousels on the desks of many executives these days, but you will find them on the vanities of some bracelet owners.

SECRETARY'S DAY
BOUQUET
bracelet

Since 1952, office workers everywhere have been celebrating a major holiday called Administrative Professionals' Day, rivaled only by the real biggies like Christmas and Easter. Usually on the third or fourth Wednesday of April, secretaries across the land are showered with chocolates, free lunches and bouquets of flowers. This bracelet is my take on the traditional bouquet.

TAKE A MEMO

In 1952, a very wise man by the name of Harry F. Klemfuss created National Secretaries Week. Klemfuss recognized how fundamental and yet undervalued administrative assistants were to the office environment. Harry was trying to spread the gospel to the world about how important workers in the secretarial/administrative field truly are and let people know they should consider careers in the field. That Harry, he really knew how to make a gal or a guy feel special for a week in April.

There is no reason the office celebration should stop in April. Just look at all these other holidays that could be observed all year long!

January 23, National Handwriting Day: After all, good penmanship is as important as typing a bazillion words a minute.

January 31, Scotch Tape Day: This is a good day to try the Paper Clip Necklace project (see page 46).

March 3–9 (date varies), Employee Appreciation Day: You should pretty much demand free lunch and flowers in April and in March.

May 16–22 (date varies), Bike-to-Work Day: Have you heard of a little thing called global warming?

May 21, National Memo Day: Her's hoping you practiced a lot back in January on National Handwriting Day.

First Friday in June, National Donut Day: Nothing will make you the office favorite quicker than bringing in a box of donuts.

July 5, Workaholic's Day: This specific holiday is against my personal beliefs, so I don't observe it.

August 18, You're a Poet and Didn't Know It: Compose some prose on the down low about how your job blows.

September 22, American Business Woman Day: This is bigger than Christmas around our house.

October 16, National Boss Day: I guess they deserve their own special day, too.

October 27, Cranky Coworker Day: Tell the office bully how you really feel about him or her today.

December 9, Homemade Gift Day: With the office holiday party right around the corner, it's a great time to think about handmade gifts.

SIGN HERE

skill level:
RUNNING THE SHOW

STUFF YOU'LL NEED

cha-cha expansion bracelet

a large selection of vintage plastic flower beads in lots of different colors

a large selection of small beads for the flower centers in lots of different colors

an assortment of large plastic beads and charms

additional charms and beads in all shapes, sizes and colors

lots and lots of head pins

lots of jump rings

round-nose pliers

chain-nose pliers

wire cutters

HOT TIP

Step 1 reminds me of an important point in the world of revamped jewelry: You can never have too much stuff. In order to conquer a bracelet like this you need to be collecting unusual beads and charms at all times and stockpiling them.

1 MAKE A STUFF PiLE

Gather all the beads and charms (plus more so you can pick and choose) you want to use. You'll also need head pins and jump rings. Remember: The more random and colorful your bracelet, the better!

2 MAKE STACKED FLOWER CHARMS

Slide a small bead and 3 vintage plastic flower beads in ascending size onto a head pin. Make a wrapped loop above the last and largest flower petal with round-nose pliers. Repeat to make about 15 or 20 stacked flower charms. (See page 18 for complete instructions on making a wrapped loop.)

3 BEGiN TO MAKE BEADED CHARM

Slide a small bead and a large bead onto a head pin and grab the wire about ⅛" (3mm) above the bead with round-nose pliers.

4 MAKE A WRAPPED LOOP ABOVE BEAD

Bend the wire around the round-nose pliers and make a wrapped loop above the beads. You are going to need oodles of these. Start by making approximately 25, and make more as needed.

5 FINISH BEADED-HEAD-PIN CHARM

Trim away any excess wire with wire cutters and straighten the loop by sandwiching it between the pincers of chain-nose pliers, if necessary.

6 BEGIN LINKING CHARMS TO BRACELET

Slide a stacked flowers charm onto a jump ring and link it to an empty ridge in the bracelet blank. (See page 19 for instructions on opening and closing a jump ring.)

7 FINISH FILLING BRACELET BLANK WITH CHARMS

Continue linking charms and dangles to the bracelet blank with jump rings. Be sure to space out your array of beads, charms and flower bouquets. The fuller the bracelet begins to get, the more difficult it will be to reach the empty spaces. At this point, you might stretch the bracelet a bit in order to reach empty ridges. Fill to max capacity.

SECRETARY'S DAY
bouquet necklace

Whether it's a holiday like Secretary's Day or just the second Tuesday in March, ladies love receiving flowers. Why not expand your bouquet-jewelry-making horizons and make a matching necklace?

TO A GREAT SECRETARY
necklace

Sometimes the search for the ultimate jewelry supply can take you into the dirty stalls of faraway flea markets, down the aisles of home-improvement stores and into your local bakery supply shop. Bake a cake for the office break room, but save the fun cake topper for your new necklace.

skill level:
YOU DESERVE A RAISE

1 SECURE FLOWERS TO PENDANT

Drill 1 hole in each of the top corners of the cake topper. Slide a black-and-white bead (or other smaller bead), a small orange flower, a medium blue flower and a larger yellow flower onto a head pin. Slide the head pin through a hole, bringing the back of the stacked flowers flush with the front of the pendant.

2 WRAP HEAD-PIN WIRE TO SECURE FLOWERS

Use your fingers to bend the head-pin wire up around the top of the pendant, then make a wrapped loop at the base of the stacked flowers. Trim away any excess wire with wire cutters. (See page 18 for instructions on making a wrapped loop.)

3 LINK PINK CHAIN TO PENDANT

Attach one end of one of the pink chains to the looped head-pin wire with a jump ring. Repeat for the other chain length. Link a lobster clasp to one of the free chain ends with a jump ring. Finish the necklace by linking 1 final jump ring to the remaining free end of pink chain. (See page 19 for instructions on opening and closing jump rings.)

margarita cake

As the saying goes: It's always five o' clock somewhere. So feel completely OK with having this cake at any time of day.

INGREDIENTS

Cake

- 1 package (18.25 ounces) orange cake mix
- 1 package (3.4 ounces) instant vanilla pudding mix
- 4 eggs
- ½ cup vegetable oil
- ⅔ cup water
- ¼ cup lemon juice
- ¼ cup tequila
- 2 tablespoons triple sec liqueur

Icing

- 1 cup confectioner's sugar
- 1 tablespoon tequila
- 2 tablespoons triple sec liqueur
- 2 tablespoons lime juice
- 2 tablespoons grated lime peel

DIRECTIONS

1. Preheat oven to 350° F. Grease and flour a cake pan, or make cupcakes (less spillage on your desk!).

2. In a large bowl, combine cake mix, pudding mix, eggs, oil, water, lemon juice, ¼ cup tequila and 2 tablespoons triple sec. Beat for 2 minutes.

3. Pour batter into prepared pan. Bake for 45 to 50 minutes (less time for cupcakes). Cool in pan for 10 minutes.

4. The icing on the cake is the extra-yummy part. In a bowl, combine lime zest, confectioner's sugar, 1 tablespoon tequila, 2 tablespoons triple sec and lime juice. Add more sugar to thicken. Mix until smooth and drizzle on cake.

Computer-related eyestrain affects oodles of diligent office workers every day. You can take "eye breaks" often and blink a lot to help the strain, or just break down and get computer glasses like I did. There is something to be said for a little Specs Appeal around the office.

SPECS APPEAL
necklace

TAKE A MEMO

Perhaps you have a pair of old glasses, but the frames are not quite cute enough to be made into a necklace to show the world. Don't fret. You still can make it work by making the glasses into a brooch!

Put your old glasses in some hot water to help pop out the lenses. Next, choose an image to place in the lens. You can use a photograph, as I did for the necklace, or perhaps an old card or piece of junk mail. Trace around the lens on top of your image as well as on top of a piece of felt, and cut out both pieces. Adhere the image to the inside of the lens with découpage medium. Feel free to use more than one image to create a mini collage! Keep an eye peeled (no pun intended) for air bubbles between the paper and glass, and gently press them out with your fingers. Next, attach your craft felt to the back of the image using a strong clear glue. Use the glue to attach the pin back.

If you are feeling really fancy, you can finish off the edge where the felt, image and glass meet with a narrow ribbon. Note: You also could use resin to make little lens brooches just as you did with the eyeglass necklace.

If all this is too much trouble, find the local branch of your Lions Club and donate your old eyeglasses to Lions Recycle for Sight. According to the World Health Organization (WHO), about 153 million people have vision problems that easily could be corrected with a little specs appeal.

STUFF YOU'LL NEED

1 pair of vintage children's glasses with lenses intact

2 images to fit lenses

6 vintage plastic flower beads (2 small pink, 2 medium turquoise, 2 large cream)

2 small silver dog charms

2 small silver flowers

6 pink plastic rings

8 turquoise channel chains

6 extra-large silver-tone jump rings

12 large silver-tone jump rings

2 silver-tone eye pins

1 silver-tone S clasp

resin and catalyst

plastic cup and wooden craft stick for mixing resin

eyeglass repair kit

scissors

high-speed drill with small drill bit

round-nose pliers

chain-nose pliers

wire cutters

127

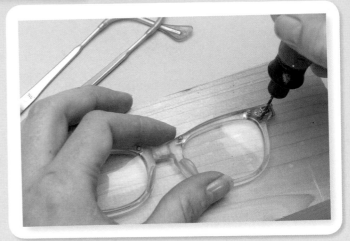

1 REMOVE ARMS FROM GLASSES

Use the screwdriver from an eyeglass repair kit to remove the arms from a pair of vintage children's glasses.

2 DRILL HOLES IN FRAME

Use a high-speed drill and a small bit to drill a hole in each side of the frame, approximately ¼" (6mm) down from where the arms were attached. (See page 21 for instructions on working with a high-speed drill.)

HORN-RIMMED GLASSES *brooch*

STUNNA SHADEZ *earrings*

Eyewear for dolls also works nicely as jewelry. Use some old clip-on earrings to exaggerate some cat-eye frames made into a brooch, or grab some wee little sunglasses and turn them into Stunna Shadez Earrings.

HOT TIP

You may find that a few bubbles have developed between the lens and the photo, despite your best efforts. Don't let them bother you. Resin can be a tad temperamental.

3 PLACE iMAGES iN FRAMES

Cut 2 images to fit inside the lenses. Be sure to use real photographs or images printed on thick photo paper, or the resin will darken them. Set the images aside and mix the resin and catalyst together according to the manufacturer's instructions. (See page 74 for the entire process.) Pour a small amount of resin into each lens. Blow on it to release the gases and pop the little bubbles. Let this bit of resin set up until it is thick and a little gooey. Smoosh each picture image-side down into the resin, making sure the resin has spread evenly between the picture and the glass lens. Use a craft stick to press and smooth the back of the photo to work out any bubbles that may have formed between the glass and the image. A little resin should ooze up around the edges of the picture. Let this layer dry. Mix a new batch of resin and pour it over the back of each photo, making sure it seals the edges. Let the glasses sit for 24 hours, allowing the resin to harden completely.

4 SECURE FLOWERS TO FRAMES

When your resin has set up, you can adorn your lenses further with flowers and charms! Link a silver dog charm to 1 of the eye pins, then thread on a small silver flower, a small pink flower, a medium turquoise flower and a large cream-colored flower. Thread the eye pin through one of the holes drilled in the frame. Secure the flowers by making a wrapped loop at the back of the frames using round-nose pliers. Trim away the excess wire with wire cutters. (See page 18 for instructions on making a wrapped loop.)

5 LINK CHAINS TO FRAMES

Beginning and ending with a turquoise channel chain, link channels and pink rings together with large jump rings until you have used 4 turquoise channels. Repeat to make a second chain. (See page 19 for instructions on opening and closing jump rings.) Link 1 chain to the wrapped loop at the back of the frames with an extra-large jump ring. Repeat for the second chain and remaining loop. Link 1 clasp component to each end of the necklace with a chain of 2 extra-large jump rings.

PUPPY DOG EYES
necklace

Even children's glasses with missing lenses make a cute necklace!

STUFF YOU'LL NEED

1 pair of vintage children's glasses with lenses removed

2 white plastic dog charms

2 large silver-tone jump rings

beads of your choice

1 silver-tone S clasp

2 36" (91cm) strands of stringing wire (work with doubled strands)

2 head pins

2 silver-tone crimp tubes

chain-nose pliers

round-nose pliers

wire cutters

high-speed drill with small drill bit

Use your drill to make small holes at the top center of each lens hole. Insert a jump ring into each hole and dangle a small charm into the spaces where the lenses once were. In this case, I used vintage Scottie Cracker Jack charms. When you remove the arms from glasses, you're left with half of the hinges still attached to the glasses (the other half was attached to the arms). Use a head pin to make a wire-wrapped loop through the hole in each hinge attached to the glasses. Attach traditional necklace strands to these loops using beads and stringing wire. Secure the ends with a clasp and crimp beads.

Needless to say, a typewriter-ribbon tin in this day and age is an archaic relic. If only replacement ink cartridges for our ink-jet printers came in such lovely little tins, office workers everywhere would look forward to filling out their material requisition forms rather than dreading it. Look for these decorative tins at flea markets and online. They come in an array of designs, including geishas, swallows, and ballerinas—all of which make lovely necklace pendants.

TYPEWRITER-RiBBON TiN *necklace*

SIGN HERE

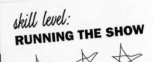

skill level:
RUNNING THE SHOW

TAKE A MEMO

Typewriter-ribbon tins also make adorable home décor items. Use them on your desk to store paper clips. Stash your breath mints in a tin for a fancy look. Make your tin into a little sewing kit, and keep it in your suitcase for emergencies.

Another fun option is to make a wee little clock. Clock mechanisms can be found at almost any major craft store or online. Find one smaller than the tin when closed. Use hands that won't extend beyond the edge of the tin. Use your awl and drill to make a hole smack in the center of your tin. The hole should be wide enough to accommodate the clock parts. Open your tin and install the clock mechanism according to the manufacturer's instructions. Close the tin. Use a strong glue to attach a large magnet to the back of your tin. When the glue dries, stick your new magnet clock on your fridge or on the side of a metal filing cabinet. If you want to use it on your desk, just set it on a small easel.

STUFF YOU'LL NEED

decorative typewriter-ribbon tin

8 typewriter-key beads

8 1" (3cm) diameter flat round black beads

16 small round red plastic beads

2 approx. 40" (102cm) lengths of .018" (.5mm) stringing wire

2 gold-tone head pins

2 gold-tone crimp tubes

1 gold-tone S clasp

nail

hammer

high-speed drill with small drill bit and cutting attachment

round-nose pliers

chain-nose pliers

wire cutters

133

1 GATHER YOUR MATERIALS

For this project, you'll need a vintage typewriter-ribbon tin, typewriter-key beads and a selection of large and small beads to complement the ribbon tin.

2 DRILL HOLES THROUGH LID AND BASE OF RIBBON TIN

With the tin closed, use a nail and a hammer to mark your hole placement and start the holes. The holes should be centered above the design on the tin cover, about 1" (3cm) apart. Remember, the holes must go through both the bottom and lid of the tin, so you must have the tin closed for this step. Once you have gone through both the top and bottom of the tin with the nail, finish making each hole with a high-speed drill and a larger drill bit. (See page 21 for instructions on working with a high-speed drill.)

3 MAKE SLITS IN BOTTOM HALF OF TIN

Open the tin and use the high-speed drill with the cutting attachment to make 2 slits down through the top of the bottom half of the tin, ending at the holes drilled in the previous step.

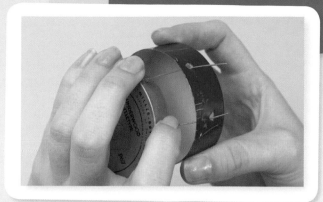

4 SLiDE HEAD PiNS THROUGH HOLES iN LiD

Slide both head pins into the slits in the bottom half of the tin so that the heads of the head pins rest inside the tin, behind their respective holes. Slide the head pins through the holes in the tin's lid, beginning from the inside of the lid so that the ends of the head pins protrude to the outside of the lid. If your drilled holes are larger than the head pins, add a small bead to the head pins inside the bottom half of the tin.

5 MAKE A WRAPPED LOOP AT TOP OF TiN

Once everything is properly aligned, close the tin completely. Make a wrapped loop in the protruding head-pin wire and trim the excess wire with wire cutters. (See page 18 for instructions on making a wrapped loop.)

7 ATTACH CLASP, AND BEAD REMAiNiNG STRAND

Bring the doubled wire through a crimp tube, through 1 of the clasp components, then back through the crimp tube. Flatten the tube with chain-nose pliers. Trim away any excess wire with wire cutters. Repeat steps 6 and 7 for the remaining beaded strand.

6 BEGiN TO BEAD WiRE

Thread a 40" (102cm) length of stringing wire through 1 of the head-pin loops. Double the wire to make a 20" (51cm) double strand. Begin to bead the wire in the following sequence, bringing both strands of wire through all the beads: typewriter key, red bead, black bead, red bead. Repeat the sequence 4 times, ending with a red bead.

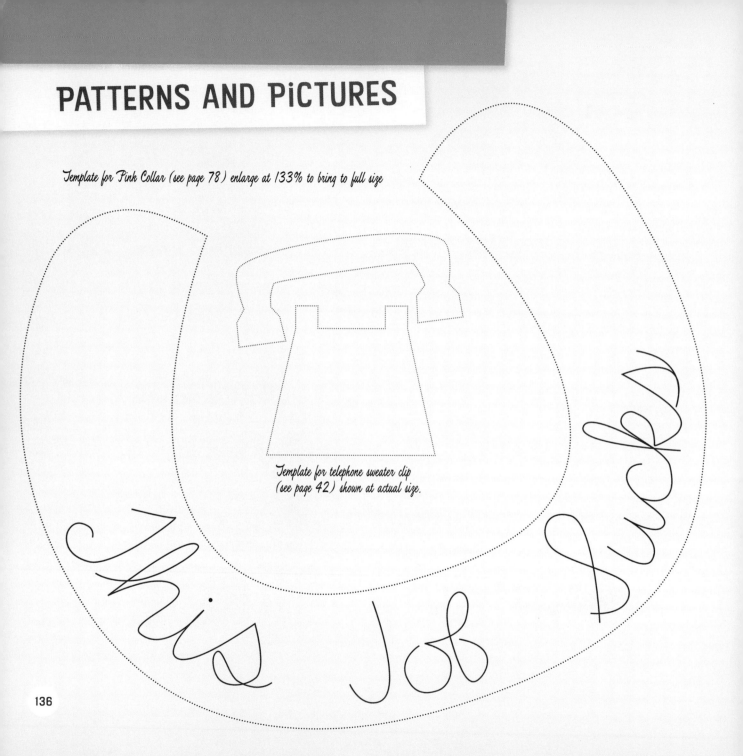

Template for Pink Collar (see page 78) enlarge at 133% to bring to full size

Template for telephone sweater clip (see page 42) shown at actual size.

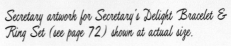

Secretary artwork for Secretary's Delight Bracelet &
Ring Set (see page 72) shown at actual size.

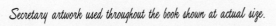

Secretary artwork used throughout the book shown at actual size.

EVERYBODY'S
blogging for the weekend!

Reading and writing blogs are two of the best ways to make the time between nine and five fly by—and help the weekend get here in a jiffy. Here are a few of my favorite blogs...

52 PROJECTS
www.52projects.com

BITS AND BOBBINS
www.bitsandbobbins.com/journal

CLAUDINE HELLMUTH
www.claudinehellmuth.blogspot.com

COQUETTE
www.coquette.blogs.com

CRAFT MAFIA
www.craft-mafia.blogspot.com

CRAFTYCHICA
www.craftychica.com/blogs/diary

CUTE OVERLOAD
www.cuteoverload.com

DECOR8
www.decor8.blogspot.com

DESIGN×SPONGE
www.designspongeonline.com

FLY: FABULOUSLY CREATIVE
www.flygirls.typepad.com/fly

FRED FLARE
www.fredflare.com/blog

GO FUG YOURSELF
www.gofugyourself.typepad.com

HAMBLY SCREEN PRINTS
www.hamblyscreenprints.typepad.com

HANDMADE DETROIT
www.handmadedetroit.com

MARGOT POTTER (A.K.A. THE IMPATIENT BLOGGER)
www.margotpotter.blogspot.com

MODISH
www.modish.typepad.com

MY OWN...
Naughty Secretary Club
www.naughtysecretaryclub.blogspot.com

PEREZ HILTON
www.perezhilton.com

POSIE GETS COZY
www.rosylittlethings.typepad.com

WEST COAST CRAFTY
www.westcoastcrafty.wordpress.com

WHIP UP
www.whipup.net

RESOURCES

Most of the supplies used to make the projects in this book can be found in your local craft, hobby, bead or discount department store. If you have trouble locating a specific product, contact one of the supply sources listed below to find a local or Internet vendor or to request a catalog. Shop at flea markets, antiques stores, hardware stores, bakeries and wherever else you happen to find yourself to pick up one-of-a-kind tchotchkes and other doodads to add to your jewelry.

A. BEL EMPORIUM
www.abelemporium.etsy.com
gnome and deer cupcake toppers

BEADALON
www.beadalon.com
beading wire

BRIMFIELD ANTIQUE SHOW
www.brimfieldshow.com
If it's worth the trip from Texas to Massachusetts, you know it's worth it.

BUZZARD BRAND
www.thebuzzardbrand.com
vintage charms, cameos, notions and more!

DREMEL
www.dremel.com
high-speed drills and bits

DUNCAN
www.duncancrafts.com
Aleene's Fabric Fusion, Liquid Fusion, Aleene's Instant Découpage Sealer & Finish, glitter

EBAY
www.ebay.com
You never know what kitschy treasure you will find.

ENVIRONMENTAL TECHNOLOGY INC.
www.eti-usa.com
resin supplies

ETSY
www.etsy.com
vintage beads and findings

HAMBLY STUDIOS
www.hamblyscreenprints.com
rub-ons (Out on a Limb, Dingbats and Robots, Vintage Letters and Stamp Alphabet)

JUDIKINS
www.judikins.com
Diamond Glaze

JUNE TAILOR
www.junetailor.com
computer-printer fabric

MAKING MEMORIES
www.makingmemories.com
brads and eyelets

MARBURGER FARM ANTIQUE SHOW
www.roundtop-marburger.com
I scheduled my wedding around this twice-annual flea market.

METALLIFEROUS
www.metalliferous.com
brass stampings and fun vintage jewelry parts

M&J TRIMMING
www.mjtrim.com
buttons and ribbon

NAUGHTY SECRETARY CLUB
www.naughtysecretaryclub.etsy.com
crafty curios and various vintage jewelry-making supplies

OFFICE DEPOT
www.officedepot.com
rulers, retractable badge holders

ORIENTAL TRADING COMPANY
www.orientaltrading.com
typewriter-key beads and watch faces

RANGER INDUSTRIES INC.
www.rangerink.com
Melting Pot, Mold-n-Pour, UTEE Flex, UTEE Brightz

RINGS & THINGS
www.rings-things.com
jewelry findings galore!

SUBLIME STITCHING
www.sublimestitching.com
everything you need to get started embroidering

UNLIKELY SOURCES

A bead store would seem like the obvious first stop for a jewelry designer, right? Truth is, I can't tell you the last time I was inside one. Sure, you need to get your beading wire, head pins and jump rings somewhere, but there's no fun in that.

Naughty Secretary Club is built on the concept that if it will sit still long enough, it may very well become a piece of jewelry. Shopping for those key pieces does not always mean a trip to the bead store. More often than not, it means rubbing elbows with housepainters or snow-globe collectors.

At every store, market and sale, always ask yourself, "What can it be?" The question "What is it?" just isn't relevant.

FLEA MARKETS, THRIFT STORES, ANTIQUES SHOPS AND GARAGE SALES

This is your new mantra: I never met a flea market I didn't like. Do a little research to learn the flea market schedules in your area. You also could be like me and jump on a plane to get to markets in other states.

Go into every antiques mall and thrift store you see, and set your alarm on Saturdays for garage sales. These are the places where you are going to find one-of-a-kind jewelry items. Look for things like old necklaces you can salvage for interesting beads, small toys you can drill for large pendants, non-working watches for bracelets, and more. Trust your instincts. If it catches your eye and you think it has potential, pay the $1.50 and take that baby home. It might take you three years to decide what you are going to do with those quilting yo-yos, but when the mood hits, you will be thankful you have them.

TEACHER SUPPLY STORES

Surprisingly, teacher supply stores are havens of crafty goodness. The one here in Austin is even called Teacher Heaven, and it might as well be called jewelry-designer heaven, as well. Small toys used to help children learn to count make wonderful bases for rings. Plus, teacher supply stores have better selections of felt than craft stores do. You could spend hours cruising the aisles of these stores and never get bored. You go in looking for jewelry supplies, and you leave with a three-foot-tall picture of Abraham Lincoln to hang in your office.

HARDWARE STORES

I never miss an opportunity to go to a hardware store. I walk in the door, tell my husband to run his errands, and then I aimlessly wander the aisles waiting for inspiration to hit. A field trip like this is where the idea for the Thank You for Calling Bangles (see page 30) came from. I have used industrial chain more times than I can count (same chain the jewelry stores carry, and most times it's a lot cheaper). There also is an entire section devoted to high-speed drills and their little accoutrements. You can find every conceivable attachment and gizmo you ever wanted or didn't know you wanted until you saw it. Don't buy expensive metal-sanding tools for the Tin Typewriter Bracelet (page 98) from a jewelry supply store—get them at the hardware store.

CRAFT STORES

You are thinking, "Duh." I'm not talking about the jewelry aisle in your craft store—I mean the entire store. I discovered the ribbon for the Quitting Time Headband (page 64) in the floral department. The base for Phoning Flo (page 56) was over with the wood cutouts. The eyelets on the Tin Typewriter Bracelet (page 98) once called the scrapbooking aisle home. Don't be afraid to explore your local craft store. Don't just run in, hit your usual jewelry section and run out. This is not how jewelry creativity happens.

THE INTERNET

It's 2 a.m. and you can't sleep. What's an aspiring jewelry designer to do? Shop for supplies on the Internet, of course. eBay is like a giant flea market/garage sale/ estate sale/bead store all rolled into one. Search the Web site using terms such as *vintage toys*, *vintage jewelry*, *vintage jewelry part* or just *beads* (this will bring up an overwhelming number of items, so you'll need to be more specific as to color, material, etc.). Don't limit yourself to eBay, however. Put different terms into your search engine and see where it takes you. Etsy is my new favorite jewelry supply store!

ETHNIC MARKETS

You can find jewelry and objects to take apart and reuse that you may not see in mainstream retail outlets. Be sure to check out ethnic grocery stores, too. Often, you can find wonderful graphics printed on food labels. Printed aluminum cans also can be cut up and made into bracelets, links and pendants. And who knows what mysterious little snack might find its way into a resin cube?

iNDEX

A–B

A Case of the Mondays, 22–59
About the Author, 5
All-Access Pass Badge
    Holder, 90
Babies and Pills Bracelet, 73
bacon and eggs, 42
bangles *See* bracelets
    and bangles
Binder-Folder Bling
    earrings, 49
    flower brooches, 51
    Necklace, 48
blanket stitch, 93
Blogs, 138
bracelets and bangles
    Babies and Pills, 73
    Clock Watcher, 85
    Happy Hour Charm, 104
    Office Hanky-Panky, 24
    Ruler, 41
    Secretary's Day
        Bouquet, 120
    Secretary's Delight, 72
    Shredded Junk Mail, 36
    Spell-Check, 29
    Thank You for Calling, 30
    Tin Typewriter, 98
    Transfer Me, 70
brooches
    Flower, 51
    Horn-Rimmed Glasses, 128
    Tied Down, 94
button-covered jewelry, 24–28
    See also Office Hanky-Panky
    Jewelry Set

C–F

cake toppers, 62, 63, 124
Casual Friday T-Shirt
    Necklace, 108
children's eyeglasses,
    repurposing, 127, 131
cinematic secretaries, 95
Clickity Clack Shoe Clips, 52
Clock Watcher
    Bracelet, 85
    Earrings, 85
    Necklace, 82
coffee filters, uses for, 107
Copy Machine Necklace, 86
Crumpled Paper Brooches, 37
deer earrings, 63
dollhouse furniture, 115
earrings
    Binder-Folder Bling, 49
    Clock Watcher, 85
    Jot-'Em-Down, 40
    Junk Food, 107
    No. 2 Earrings, 40
    Office Hanky-Panky, 27
    Phone Cord, 33
    Stunna Shadez, 129
    Transfer Me, 70
    Whistle at Work, 63
Everybody's Blogging for the
    Weekend!, 138 *See also*
    Web sites
File Sweater Clips, 43
Flower Brooches, 51
Flower Combs, 79

G–L

gnomes, 62–63
hair accessories
    Button-Covered Hair Ties, 28
    Flower Combs, 79
    Quitting Time Headband, 64
    Tie One On Headbands, 69
    Vanity Hair Comb, 118
Happy Hour Charm Bracelet, 104
harvesting metal, 99
Heart Earrings, 49 *See also*
    Binder-Folder Bling
Horn-Rimmed Glasses
    Brooch, 128
Hotel Key Necklace, 112
Hump Day, 60–101
I Heart You Sweater Clip, 44
Introduction, 8
Job Skills, 10
Jot-'Em-Down Earrings, 40
Junk Food Jewelry, 107

M–N

Making a Wrapped Loop, 18
Margarita Cake, 125
Nameplate Necklace, 87
necklaces
    Binder-Folder Bling, 48
    Button-Covered, 27
    Casual Friday T-Shirt, 108
    Clock Watcher, 82
    Copy Machine, 86
    Hotel Key, 112
    Nameplate, 87

Paper Clip, 46
Pencil Pusher, 34
Pencil on a Ball Chain, 35
Phoning Flo, 56
Puppy Dog Eyes, 131
Secretary's Day
    Bouquet, 120
Secretary's Pad, 114,
    118, 119
Shredded Junk Mail, 38
Specs Appeal, 126
Swizzle Stick, 105
To a Great Secretary, 124
Typewriter-Ribbon Tin, 132
Whistle at Work, 62
No. 2 Earrings, 40

O–R

Office Hanky-Panky Jewelry Set, 24
    bracelet, 24
    earrings, 27
    necklace, 27
    ring, 27
office holidays, 121
office romance survey, 25
Opening and Closing a
    Jump Ring, 19
Paper Clip Necklace, 46
Patterns and Pictures, 136
Payday Jewelry, 111
Pencil on a Ball Chain, 35
Pencil Pusher Necklace, 34
Phone Cord Earrings, 33
Phoning Flo Necklace, 56
Pink Collar, 78
Puppy Dog Eyes Necklace, 131
Quitting Time Headband, 64
Ravishing Receptionist
    Sweater Clips, 42
resin projects
    Secretary's Delight Bracelet
        and Ring Set, 72
    Specs Appeal Necklace, 126

Resources, 139
rings
    Office Hanky-Panky, 27
    We Need a Raise, 29
    Secretary's Delight, 72
Ruler Bracelet, 41

S–Z

secretary images, 91, 137
Secretary School, 18
Secretary's Day Bouquet
    Bracelet, 120
    Necklace, 123
Secretary's Delight Bracelet
    and Ring Set, 72
Secretary's Pad
    more jewelry, 118
    Necklace, 114, 118, 119
shoe clips
    Clickity Clack, 52
    Typewriter Key, 55
Shredded Junk Mail
    Bangles, 36
    Earrings, 36, 38
    Necklace, 38
Skill levels See Job Skills
Specs Appeal Necklace, 126
Spell-Check Bracelets, 29
stamp carousel, 119
Stunna Shadez Earrings, 129
Supplies, 12
    nontraditional, 14
    traditional jewelry-
        making, 12
sweater clips
    bacon and eggs, 42
    File, 43
    I Heart You, 44
    Ravishing Receptionist, 42
    Vintage, 45
Swizzle Stick Necklace, 105
T-shirt, Naughty Secretary
    Club, 109

Techniques See Secretary School
TGIF, 102–135
Thank You for Calling
    Bangles, 30
Things You Can Do with a High-
    Speed Drill, 20
Tie One On Headbands, 69
Tied Down Brooch, 94
Tin Typewriter Bracelet, 98
To a Great Secretary
    Necklace, 124
Tools, 16
Transfer Me Jewelry, 70
    bangles, 70
    earrings, 70
    pendants, 71
Typewriter Belt Buckle, 101
Typewriter Key Shoe Clips, 55
Typewriter-Ribbon Tin
    Necklace, 132
Unlikely Sources, 140
Vanity Hair Comb, 118
vintage paper clip necklace, 46
Vintage Sweater Clip, 45
We Need a Raise Ring, 29
Web sites, 65, 67, 138
whipstitch, 93
Whistle at Work
    Earrings, 63
    Necklace, 62

LEARN TO MAKE MORE
COOL CRAFTY STUFF
WiTH THESE OTHER *North Light titles!*

PLUSH YOU!
BY KRISTEN RASK

This showcase of 100 plush toys will inspire you to join in the DIY toy phenomenon. Making these plushies is so fun and easy—it's instant gratification for beginners plus great inspiration for experienced toy makers. Stuffed space creatures and lovable monsters, along with the occasional cut of beef and other squeezable subjects, make this an irresistibly hip book you'll just want to hug.

ISBN-10: 1-58180-996-4
ISBN-13: 978-1-58180-996-1
paperback, 144 pages, Z0951

PLEXi CLASS
BY TONIA DAVENPORT

Flip through the pages of *Plexi Class*, and you'll see plastic in a whole new light. This book shows you how to take ordinary plastic—including Plexiglas, vinyl and even shrink plastic—and combine it with mixed-media elements to make beautiful jewelry and accessories. Author Tonia Davenport teaches you all the skills you need to cut and shape Plexiglas into earrings, charms, pendants, and even totes and boxes, with a modern, industrial look.

ISBN-10: 1-60061-061-7
ISBN-13: 978-1-60061-061-5
paperback, 128 pages, Z1753

SPARKLETASTiC
BY MARGOT POTTER

The time has come for you to break out the glitter and release your inner diva! *Sparkletastic* gives you more than 40 fabulous jewelry pieces and accessories to wear when you want to sparkle. Get ready for a glamorous adventure to a glittery wonderland where a crystal tiara is part of the everyday dress code and a rhinestone-studded lunchbox is a necessary accessory. Viva la sparkle!

ISBN 13: 978-1-58180-973-2
ISBN 10: 1-58180-973-5
paperback, 128 pages, Z0759

CANVAS REMiX
BY ALISA BURKE

Learn how to bring graffiti art off the street and onto canvas to make everything from wall hangings to bracelets and bags. Inside *Canvas Remix*, you'll find more than 40 techniques for combining paint, collage and canvas in totally unexpected ways. Creating graffiti-inspired art may not give you instant street cred, but once you've mastered these techniques, your finished pieces are sure to turn heads.

ISBN 13: 978-1-60061-075-2
ISBN 10: 1-60061-075-7
paperback, 128 pages, Z1844

These books and other fine North Light titles are available at your local craft retailer, bookstore or online supplier. Or visit our Web site at www.mycraftivity.com.